ROUTLEDGE LIBRARY EDITIONS: URBAN HISTORY

Volume 6

SIGNS OF CHANGE

SIGNS OF CHANGE
Urban Iconographies in San Francisco, 1880–1915

RON ROBIN

Taylor & Francis Group
LONDON AND NEW YORK

First published in 1990 by Garland Publishing Ltd.

This edition first published in 2018
by Routledge
2 Park Square, Milton Park, Abingdon, Oxon OX14 4RN

and by Routledge
711 Third Avenue, New York, NY 10017

Routledge is an imprint of the Taylor & Francis Group, an informa business

© 1990, Ron T. Robin

All rights reserved. No part of this book may be reprinted or reproduced or utilised in any form or by any electronic, mechanical, or other means, now known or hereafter invented, including photocopying and recording, or in any information storage or retrieval system, without permission in writing from the publishers.

Trademark notice: Product or corporate names may be trademarks or registered trademarks, and are used only for identification and explanation without intent to infringe.

British Library Cataloguing in Publication Data
A catalogue record for this book is available from the British Library

ISBN: 978-0-8153-5316-4 (Set)
ISBN: 978-1-351-13718-8 (Set) (ebk)
ISBN: 978-0-8153-4924-2 (Volume 6) (hbk)
ISBN: 978-1-351-13750-8 (Volume 6) (ebk)

Publisher's Note
The publisher has gone to great lengths to ensure the quality of this reprint but points out that some imperfections in the original copies may be apparent.

Disclaimer
The publisher has made every effort to trace copyright holders and would welcome correspondence from those they have been unable to trace.

SIGNS OF CHANGE

•

*Urban
Iconographies in
San Francisco,
1880–1915*

•

Ron Robin

GARLAND PUBLISHING • NEW YORK & LONDON • 1990

Copyright © 1990 by Ron Robin
All Rights Reserved

Library of Congress Cataloging-in-Publication Data

Robin, Ron Theodore.
Signs of change: urban iconographies in San Francisco, 1880-1915/ Ron Robin.
p. cm. — (European immigrants and American society)
Includes bibliographical references.
ISBN 0-8240-0317-9 (alk. paper)
1. San Francisco (Calif.)—History. 2. Immigrants—California—San Francisco—History. 3. Urbanization—California—San Francisco—History. 4. San Francisco (Calif.)—Maps, Mental. I. Title. II. Series
F869.S357R63 1990
979.4'61—dc20   90—3506

●

Printed on acid-free, 250-year-life paper.
Manufactured in the United States of America

Design by
Julie Threlkeld

Table of Contents

Preface..i

Acknowledgments...v

Introduction...1

1. The Civic Image of the Forty-niner as
   "Para-History" of San Francisco 9

2. San Francisco Smelting Pot 43

3. San Francisco's Jews and the Architecture
   of Symbolic Ethnicity...70

4. Ambivalent Heroes; Icons of Self-Image
   Among San Francisco's Italians..106

5. Epilogue 145

6. Bibliographical Essay...152

PREFACE

In his *Conquest of America*, Tzvetan Todorov identifies the crystallization of a systematic understanding of the unfamiliar—"the perception of the other"—with the proliferation of writing.[1] The pen, an "evolution in the technology of symbolism" furnishes observers with a didactic tool for fathoming societies far removed from their world in both time and space. In turn, the understanding of "the other" is sought, first and foremost, through the subject's written documents. When faced with a variety of sources—archeological, quantitative, or verbal—the choice invariably falls upon the written record as the primary means for reconstructing distant cultures. Problems arise, however, when the power of language as a common denominator diminishes. In periods of transition and flux, when access to the written word is impaired or when polyglot cultures are thrust together in fortuitous circumstances, documents do not always reflect the sentiments of broad cross sections of society. This particular problem characterizes evaluations of urbanization in the United States.

Most written descriptions of urban expansion in America present pictures of a landscape wrought with strife and corruption. In dramatic descriptions of clashes between immigrants and the native born, workers and businessmen, saloon politicos and affluent crusaders, the city is invariably characterized as the loser. With few exceptions, urban America as an Eden wasted by conflict, greed, and incompetence, dominates both contemporary descriptions and historical analyses of the city between two centuries.

And yet, as Jon C. Teaford notes, "nagging realities stand in stark contrast to the traditional tableau" of irreconcilable strife and the ensuing paralysis of the city.[2] An unequalled system of water supply, imaginative sewerage systems, lavish parks, monumental bridges; all these artifacts of urban achievement were the result of cooperative ventures between seemingly irreconcilable enemies and sub-cultures. Urban achievements belie the picture of disarray and incapacitating antagonisms. The amenities and monuments which covered metropolitan America, from San Francisco to New York, were the products of compromise, the progenitors of collaboration—no matter how uneasy—between wary urbanites.

This sense of compromise and shared goals cannot be derived effortlessly from written material. A pugnacious press, bent on selling newspapers through aggressive reporting, made headlines out of every urban fault, while evidence of mundane cooperative achievements lay buried in the back pages. The upper middle class, whose access to the written word eclipsed all efforts at articulation among other city people, complained the loudest. Unhappy with the need to rub shoulders with upstart immigrants, uncouth workers, and unrefined shopkeepers, middle class essayists often ignored the pragmatic accomplishments of heterogeneous and polyglot city dwellers.

The following pages probe the expression of common denominators among urbanites through the fashioning of their communal symbols. Assessing city people according to their own demonstrative standards and through the visual images by which they wished to be remembered is the focus of this study. Within this context, special attention is devoted to the visual perceptions of immigrants, those whose senses were not smothered by over-familiarity or protracted compliance with American mores. All too often, immigration histories concentrate exclusively on narrow connections between newcomers and their urban surroundings. With few exceptions, the city in immigration studies is approached as being in conflict with immigrant values. At best, the city has served as data-base for the study of specific immigrant communities; frequently, it has provided mere background for cloistered studies of immigrant life.

Immigrant assessments of urban culture beyond the ghetto have been overlooked partly because of over-reliance on written documents. What we cannot read, we cannot see. Ethnic newspapers and novels in English written by immigrants and their children have furnished most of the sources for historical studies of newcomers in the American city. Concentration on the ghetto experience is an inherent quality of the immigrant novel. The ethnic press and its singular mission of maintaining a sense of group consciousness also avoided objective appraisals of the American city, the nemesis of immobile ethnicity.

But urban immigrants should not be approached only as a source for unearthing their own introspective experiences; newcomers also provided windows into the special ambience of their adopted homes. Through the analysis of immigrant iconography, this investigation seeks the existence of common cultural principles in an American city.

San Francisco provides the main setting for this investigation stretching roughly from 1880 to 1915, when unprecedented urbanization coincided with an immigration of unheralded proportions. The city's morphology set it apart from other American cities where rapid growth and large concentrations of immigrants could also be found. As a comparatively new city, tested by earthquake and fire,

San Francisco's ever-changing cityscape visually documented the fortunes and fears of its inhabitants.

Immigrant iconography in San Francisco, usually found upon community buildings or displayed in ethnic ceremonies, soared above the ghetto. These visible assertations of common cultural principles in the city transcended the narrow interests of ethnic newspapers and immigrant romances. In a society where large portions of the population had a poor command of the dominant language, visual statements highlighted fundamental points of agreement among urbanites from all walks of life.

ACKNOWLEDGMENTS

This book is a revised and abbreviated version of my 1986 dissertation. As such, I take great pleasure in thanking once the Librarians and staff of the Bancroft Library at the University of California, the Western Jewish Historical Archives, Judah Magnes Museum, Berkeley, and the San Francisco Public Library. Many thanks to Marlene Getz for her wonderful photographs.

For their constructive criticism I am grateful to the members of my dissertation committee at the University of California, Berkeley: James Vance Jr., James H. Kettner, and my friend and mentor, Gunther Barth. I received much needed advice and good counseling from another good friend, Richard Polenberg of Cornell University.

University of Haifa, Israel

INTRODUCTION

"American civilization grows more hieroglyphic every day," marveled art critic Vachel Lindsay. "The cartoons ..., the advertisements in the back of magazines and on the bill- boards and in the street cars, the acres of photographs in the Sunday newspapers, make us into a hieroglyphic civilization far nearer to Egypt than to England."[1] When stripped of their hyperbole, Lindsay's observations represent an astute comment on inter-group communication in the United States between two centuries. Lindsay meant, of course, that modern American society was acutely attuned to receiving and transmitting concepts of culture through visual means, perhaps more so than through the conventional tool of writing.

In the typical large American city, polyglot people were thrust together in circumstances which severely impeded conventional verbal modes of communication. In a fluctuating world of novel thought patterns, amorphous values, and fantastic forms, the common, universal lexicon of visual images functioned as a means of communal intercourse almost by default. It stands to reason, therefore, that the deciphering of visual language in the American ambience is of particular importance, especially for students of American culture whose interests lie in unearthing some sense of a shared experience above and beyond the many divisions inherent in the United States during the age of modernization and hyper-growth.

An analysis of visual sources makes particular sense for those of us studying America's cities during the high tide of urbanization and immigration ranging roughly from the 1880s until the First World War. A significant portion of the urban population was composed of immigrants who, for all practical purposes, were functionally illiterate, at least as far as the English language was concerned. Even those who had a command of English, found that their access to print was limited, and, consequently they have left only sporadic comments on their impressions of their new home.

This work focuses, then, on the universal vernacular of pictorial form and its function as visual representations of collective cultures in urban America. Two basic methodological assumptions have provided the framework for this study. First and foremost, I have embraced Emile Durkheim's assertion that fundamental concepts and world views are not formed autonomously in each person on the basis of individual experiences, but appear to be assimilated by the individual from the culture. With these thoughts in mind, I have approached a representative cross-section of ethnic visual representations as graphic projections of collective attitudes, and not as personal, idiosyncratic expression.

In addition I have assumed that the multi-faced, multi-lingual American city can, indeed, be viewed as a composite culture. Gunther Barth has shown that American cities during the period investigated here were united by a concept of "metropolism," which he defines as the tendency to duplicate a preordained pattern of urban culture in the United States, irrespective of the vast distances which separated established eastern cities from burgeoning new cities in the west.[2] Based upon this supposition that urban Americans did, indeed, develop a collective consciousness, I have sought to discover the deliberate and methodical transposing of cardinal ideas of the composite culture into recognizable metaphors. I have avoided an over-reliance on written sources, preferring instead, the highly visible and universal, and perhaps, "primitive" language of visual representations.

These visual representations, Ernst Gombrich noted in his seminal essay on the significance of perception, are often trivialized by regarding them as mere tools of personal, introspective self-expression. We are prone to forget that art has always functioned as a medium for transforming abstract concepts of a faith into visible metaphors.[3] My criteria for the selection of visual signals have been, repetition and visibility. Each of the chapters has focused primarily on one type of visual symbol which appeared with great frequency and/or in locations or situations of high visibility. Upon identifying the fundamental cultural patterns embedded in these images, I have then traced the infiltration of dissonant elements, the gradual transformation of the symbol in accordance with shifting world views, the clashing ideologies, and mixture of thought patterns which characterized urban America during its heyday.

This exercise in reading culture through visual sources, focuses on San Francisco and its three main white ethnic groups: mainstream American-born citizens, Italians, and Jews. San Francisco provides an apt setting for studying turn-of-the-century urban culture through visual sources. Earthquakes and fires required the city to replace, periodically, much of its civic iconography. The cyclical process of rebuilding produced a genre of public and popular art which mirrored the cultural consequences of rapid expansion and incessant change.

In addition to this conscious articulation of identity through mainstream civic art, the city's large and vociferous immigrant groups also offered multiple visual signs for assessing the meeting of heterogeneous peoples. By 1890, San Francisco had the largest percentage of foreign- born residents among the thirty-five principal cities in the United States. Nearly 127,000 of the city's 299,000 inhabitants—more than forty-two percent—were foreign born. Of these, 77,000 were immigrants from non-English speaking countries.[4] Like their native counterparts, immigrants utilized public art as a means of communicating their perceptions of American urban life.

Most studies of immigrants in the United States tend to highlight the vivid collage of sub-cultures in the United States, the differences between its people. While the ever- growing examinations of distinctive qualities of immigrants has enriched our understanding of America's social and cultural texture, we have, in the process, unceremoniously dismissed the notion of a common urban culture in the United States. First introduced by Arthur Schlesinger Jr., in *The Rise of the City* (1933), the concept of common frames of reference forged by different people seeking a modicum of equilibrium in an unfamiliar and distinctively American milieu, has fallen into disrepute.[5]

It would appear that this sense of a shared culture is more easily discovered in San Francisco than anywhere else, at least as far as its white ethnic groups are concerned. To begin with, the city never had an entrenched American elite. Immigrants, and Americans from every part of the continent arrived in the city at about the same time. Moreover, the presence of oriental newcomers enhanced the feeling of a shared destiny among the city's white citizens. Much of the prejudices suffered by southern and eastern Europeans in other American cities was deflected by the Chinese, thereby freeing white immigrants psychologically from a siege mentality.

The city's two largest groups of immigrants, Jews and Italians, furnish the basis for seeking common denominators between mainstream American San Francisco and its European newcomers. The city had a flourishing Jewish community and an affluent Italian colony, both of which had firm roots in the gold rush era. Beginning in the 1880s, when San Francisco shed its petulant boom town image and became an indistinguishable element in the national-urban industrial network, established Jews and veteran Italians confronted an influx of impoverished newcomers whose very presence challenged their settled ways. As indirect comments on the vices and virtues of immigrant sub-cultures, the ensuing hagglings between Jewish and Italian notables and the ordinary immigrants spewed forth constant assessments of American mores and immigrant traditions.

4 Signs of Changes

Given the limited use of the written word in these debates between established immigrant leaders and newcomers, much of the cardinal points were transposed into visual icons, ranging from the elaborate iconography of communal buildings, to cemeteries.

The point of departure for this study is an analysis of the civic representations of the Forty-niner, California's legendary miner, and symbol of the American-born component in San Francisco. Contextual adjustments in this image reflected the winds of change that swept through the city. Initially, in the heady days of gold fever, the Forty-niner had represented equal opportunity for all persevering individuals. By the turn of the century, and with the integration of the former boom town into the nation's urban-industrial network, the hierarchy of values embodied in the miner changed in accordance with modified perceptions of social and economic opportunity. Throughout the period analyzed in this study, civic representations of the Forty- niner avoided unchanging virtues. The miner mirrored constantly changing perceptions of urban reality as well as the adjustment of expectations in accordance with the fluid environment of a vacillating urban milieu.

This Forty-niner was an integral element in a genre of civic art which was both financed and initiated by the city's established elite. Consequently, the use of this singular heroic figure as a symbol of the city may appear, at first glance, to be part of a controlled reaction of a privileged class to the heterogeneous character of urban America. Indeed, the city's large immigrant groups displayed an array of ethnic symbols which ostensibly clashed with the peculiarly California miner. Jews and Italians, perhaps the two most conspicuous groups of newcomers in American cities, produced many symbols of ethnic exceptionalism in San Francisco. Elaborate Hebraic temples, and Italian emblems drawn from the political culture of the Risorgimento, characterized their iconographical agenda.

Yet despite obvious differences in iconographical idiom and form, striking similarities of content existed between the Forty-niner as symbol of the urban establishment, and immigrant manifestations of identity in San Francisco. Even though the political symbols, ethnic signs, and cults of Italian national heroes were drawn from a distant context, these monuments of foreign origins actually signalled a departure from an isolated colonial culture. The local cult of the Risorgimento hero, Giuseppe Garibaldi, for example, gradually stopped relating its hero to the politics and internal skirmishes of Italy, and instead, focused on Garibaldi's more generic qualities of bravery and honesty as well as his years of exile in America. Simultaneously, a more malleable, urbane, and sometimes uniquely Californian version of Christopher Columbus emerged, and assumed a manner not unlike that of the Forty-niner.

Like the fluctuations in the image of the Forty-niner, transitions in Italian iconography in San Francisco acknowledged that urban culture was not an immutable formula based on static tenets, but a liquid prescription for making sense of life in a setting of rapid change. The modification of Italian cult images and their adaptation to the American context revealed a sense of identity intended to match the realities and opportunities of the urban-American setting. For San Francisco's Italians, the recalling of their collective past was an active process, not a retrieval of static images from a distant heritage. To remember meant using the past in the service of the present.

Iconographical displays among San Francisco's Jews were most conspicuously represented in their temples. Their design and decoration never relied on rigid cultural testimony, but upon formulas for smooth transition and adaptation to a process of rapid urbanization. Temples decorated with introspective pseudo-oriental signs were cast aside abruptly. Instead, Jewish temples incorporated the fashionable California mission style. Above and beyond the significance of this iconographical transition as an indicator of Jewish acculturation, the move from an ethnocentric symbolism to a synthetic historical myth of California's Hispanic origins mirrored an important aspect of urban life in America. The confusing pace of the American city demanded a usable past, one which a heterogeneous city people could adapt, change, and modify. A romantic and fictional version of California's past, which bore little resemblance to actual history, served this purpose quite adequately. The adaptation of the legend of California's golden age to a Jewish context exemplified how city dwellers manufactured relics of an imagined history in order to produce common cultural denominators in a period of rapid change.

The methodology applied in this study raises obvious queries regarding the validity of extrapolating historical trends from visual sources. As such, I have sought to verify my interpretation of cultural signs through other measurements of urban change, in particular politics. Indeed, the transition in the image of the Forty-niner, from flamboyant individual to ordinary person, resembled the shifts in the political preferences of San Franciscans in the municipal arena. The ethnic modifications of symbolic identity appear to mirror social shifts. In the case of Italians, the political tensions between veterans and "greenhorns" produced political skirmishes which corroborate the significance discovered in iconographical observations. The social impetus for alterations in the iconography of Jewish temples is explained in various congregational records and community newsletters. In addition, the popular culture of less affluent Jews in the city, those who had no such extravagant temples to register their concepts of urban life, bears a striking resemblance to the cultural signals engraved in the iconography of affluent Jewish congregations.

The relevance of the San Francisco experience to the overall American urban context remains, of course, a debatable issue. San Francisco was an "instant city," in which the entire history of American urban development was telescoped into thirty years or so. The city's immigrant experience was also quite unique. European immigrants fared comparatively well in San Francisco because a large Chinese community fielded much of the abuse reserved for Jews and Italians in other parts of the country. The city's Italians also displayed an unusual sociological profile, for unlike other American cities, most newcomers hailed from the more urbane north rather than from the feudalistic southern section of the country. Unlike the east coast experience, the city's well- established German Jews were never overwhelmed by the tidal wave of refugees from eastern Europe. A mere trickle of the impoverished Jewish migrants arrived in the San Francisco Bay area.

San Francisco, then, was not the most typical American city. However, it was probably the most expressive. An analysis of such an evasive subject as visual manifestations of the American urban mentality requires that speculation and hypotheses should be documented with vivid examples. San Francisco's lavish civic and ethnic art—the by-product of frequent rebuilding and expansion— has allowed me to establish firm connections between the social and cultural contexts of American urban life through the use of visual sources.

The urban iconography of San Francisco exemplifies the intimate interaction between mentality and reality, and the process by which meaningful frames of reference are formed for coping with urban life. As established cultural standards lost their relevance in the face of extensive change, the ensuing discrepancies between ideas and reality stimulated the creation of new symbols of culture seeking to supply the meaning that older insignia could no longer dispense. While the lexicon of symbols in San Francisco reflected the origins and traditions of a diverse people, the ideological contents of these different forms of visual expression were strikingly similar. Jewish temples, Italian national heroes, and the indigenous image of the Forty-niner all extolled flexibility over moral rigidity, and preferred expediency to the virtues of inherited standards of conduct. The San Francisco experience suggests that the divisions, tensions, and heterogeneity of urbanites in the United States did not preclude the forging of fundamental, shared cultural concepts. Even though American urbanites rarely spoke with one voice, they were all exposed to the complex system of values which was part and parcel of the communal experience of coming to terms with the American city.

8   Signs of Changes

Notes

1. Vachel Lindsay, *The Art of the Moving Picture* (New York, New Edition, 1970), 21-22. This particular edition is a reprint of Lindsay's 1922 edition and includes an introduction by Stanley Kauffmann.
2. Gunther Barth, *City People; The Rise of Modern City Culture in Nineteenth Century America* (New York, 1980), 25-26.
3. Ernst Gombrich, "The Use of Art for the Study of Symbols," in James Hogg (ed.), *Psychology and the Visual Arts* (Harmondsworth, England, 1969), 149-170. See also Gombrich's *Art History and the Social Sciences; The Romanes Lecture for 1973* (Oxford, 1975).
4. Bureau of the Census, *Eleventh Census; Abstract* (Second Revised and Enlarged Edition, Washington, D. C., 1896), 10, table 43; -----, *Compendium of the Eleventh Census, 1890*, 2 vols. (Washington, D. C., 1894), ii, 604; *ibid.*, ii, 541-580. See also Frank L. Beach, "The Effects of the Westward Movement on California's Growth and Development, " *International Migration Review*, 3 (Summer, 1969), 23.
5. Arthur Schlesinger Jr., *The Rise of the City; 1878-1898* (New York, 1933). See also Ralph E. Turner, "The Industrial City; Center of Cultural Change, " in Caroline F. Ware (ed.), *The Cultural Approach to History* (New York, 1940). The most stimulating among the few recent studies that have grappled with the notion of universal concepts of culture in the American city are Thomas Bender, *Towards an Urban Vision; Ideas and Institutions in Nineteenth Century America* (Lexington, Kentucky, 1975); Gunther Barth, *City People* (New York, 1980); John Bodnar, *The Transplanted; a History of Immigrants in Urban America* (Bloomington, Indiana, 1985).

CHAPTER 1
THE CIVIC IMAGE OF THE FORTY-NINER AS "PARA-HISTORY" OF SAN FRANCISCO

Having been exposed to endless tales concerning the cosmopolitan complexion of gold rush San Francisco, Amy Bernardy had expected to find an exotic and idiosyncratic urban center in this remote corner of American expansion. Instead, upon arriving in the city in the early years of the twentieth century, this Italian social worker and political reformer encountered a drab collection of wooden edifices, as bland as the monotonous row houses of any American city. San Francisco's cityscape, Bernardy ruefully recorded in her diary, was a vulgar reflection of the standardized commercial instincts of its polyglot inhabitants.[1]

Bernardy's disappointment derived, in part, from her scant acquaintance with the frontier tradition of tall tales and the superlatives of American boosterism. In an environment of rapid growth, the present, the future, and an imaginary past occasionally fused into a syntax of indistinct temporal boundaries. What should have been and what might yet be, often colored local perceptions of an uncertain present.[2] In addition, Bernardy was puzzled by the lack of ceremonial significance in San Francisco's cityscape, which had developed haphazardly, and without the inspiration of grand designs. As an upper middle-class European, Bernardy was attuned to classical images of the city—the Civitas—as a repository of cultural values and moral guidance. In the monotonous grid of San Francisco streets she failed to find any sense of direction from a higher source. The faceless urban countenance also challenged her perceptions of American democracy as comprised of independent citizens with singular personalities. Searching for some unique aspect of San Francisco's general appearance above its industrialized standardization, she found none. It was if some unknown conspiracy had succeeded in obliterating any sense of originality between the two coasts, she noted rather sadly.

In this sense San Francisco's supposedly drab appearance was more a function of Bernardy's pre-conceptions of a way a city should look than of reality. In the cities of emperors, kings, or other systems of strict political deference, the trappings of ceremonial order were introduced into every aspect of a controlled cityscape. By contrast, a hastily constructed San Francisco revealed a distinct

10 Signs of Changes

separation between the symbolic and the functional. San Francisco's buildings, commercial and private, were erected to meet the immediate exigencies of a rapidly growing city. Hence, San Francisco never adopted an architectural master plan based on preconceived cultural values. Instead, the city's cultural consciousness was articulated separately in isolated objects: in particular civic statues, sporadic municipal art projects, and the occasional ostentatious civic temple.

The projection of resonant symbolism through individual works of art in public places rather than through holistic urban design made particular sense in San Francisco. In the city's brief history, extraordinary expansion and the ravages of nature had promoted expedient construction methods and had discouraged costly aesthetic considerations. By 1860 a tiny outpost of Spanish colonialism had already turned into a bustling town of 56,000 inhabitants. A decade later, San Francisco housed 150,000 inhabitants. By 1890, its population had swelled to about 300,000.[3] During this period of rapid extension significant sections of the city were periodically demolished by fire and earthquake. Damaged districts were hastily reconstructed with scant attention paid to style or taste.

Under these circumstances, San Francisco's architecture represented a case study of what environmental historian J.B. Jackson has called "vernacular architecture," a provisional style of construction whose attachment to place was strictly temporary and pragmatic.[4] The ceremonial contours of San Francisco, its symbols of urban culture, were fashioned independently and superimposed upon a pre-fabricated cityscape. Over the years, the city's values were enshrined in a setting of vernacular architecture and plain streets. Instead of being an integral part of an architectural master-plan for the city, these signposts of culture occupied designated sites of high visibility, such as important cross-roads, or those areas most likely to find urbanites in a pensive mood, in particular cemeteries and houses of worship.

The most functional form of this genre of civic art was of course the individual statue. Statues represented a relatively cheap medium for signalling cultural concepts. Their maneuverability, and flexibility also enhanced their attraction. As compact works of art, they could be transferred from place to place according to shifts in urban growth and expansion. Statues could and, indeed, were removed when their inherent values lost their attractiveness. Above all, statues functioned as a form of common communication for a multi-lingual people who lacked an alternative form of sustained dialogue in the segmented

Ron Robin

city. "Picture writing from the earliest days has been man's universal language," noted Frederick S. Lamb, a leading proponent of civic art in turn-of-the-century America. "Symbols, signs, heraldry are but the shorthand of the mind, and but for the decadence of our art, would to-day supplant many needless mediums." Almost by default, statues represented the only means of exposing the "masses" and the "foreign population" of American cities to those particular middle class values which they failed to receive through "traditional written sources."[5]

Two distinctive forms of officially sanctioned civic statues appeared in the American city at the turn of the century. Well-established centers, such as New York and Chicago, mostly chose the path of enshrining political super-heroes. Their municipally-endorsed statuary was based upon pivotal national figures who were used as vehicles for sanctifying the values of those who held the reins of local power. In the "instant cities" of the far west, where the likes of a Washington or a Lincoln had never cast a giant shadow, civic art employed an alternative strategy. In order to attract public attention, statues utilized themes that could be recognized by a variety of city people, irrespective of their origins. In other words, exemplary figures were created out of the shared experiences of the cities' residents.[6]

San Francisco, an urban center composed of multi-cultural citizens with no enduring traditions to share, did not endorse the use of statues of great figures from America's eastern past. Predictably, local community leaders focused upon synthesized motifs which could appeal to the largest common denominator. The most popular theme of this particular school of ceremonial urban art in San Francisco was the California miner, the legendary Forty-niner of the gold rush. Over the years the gold seeker had become an unofficial city symbol. Having worked his way into both the civic and state seal, and with frequent appearances on street corners and in San Francisco's two large international expositions, the Forty-niner served as the most ubiquitous image of civic art in San Francisco.

In contrast to other subjects of civic art, the miner was indigenous to the area and had not been carried over in the cultural baggage of any particular segment of the city's population. In this sense, the civic image of the Forty- niner represented what Michael Grant has called "para- history," the creation and manipulation of a historical narrative which is meant to rationalize contemporary predicaments rather than trace "real" historical developments.[7] The miner's constant presence in ceremonial art provides an opportunity for evaluating elements of change and continuity in urban culture, because, despite his ubiquity,

12 Signs of Changes

his features and traits were altered significantly as San Francisco went through the motions of cramming the entire process of American urban development into some fifty years.

Of course, not all San Franciscans belonged to that particular group of fortune seekers who converged on the area during the first year of gold fever. Yet the underlying significance of the mining experience, the pursuit of individual economic gain in an environment of relatively unrestrained opportunity, continued to attract newcomers to the city even after the glitter of gold had faded. Writing in 1879, well after the decline of gold mania in California, Horatio Alger of rags-to-riches fame found universal significance in the Forty-niner experience. The success of classic mining heroes meant that "some measure of prosperity awaits the patient and energetic worker" even in the years following the gold rush.[8] As such, the civic representation of the Forty-niner, in particular the shifts in his image after the demise of gold fever, provides a unique opportunity for fathoming the changing parameters of culture in an American city during its pivotal years of consolidation.

Before analyzing the image of the Forty-niner in civic art during the period of urban consolidation from 1880 to 1915, we need to define the mythic traits of the miner as they emerged during the height of the gold rush. The pristine image of the Forty-niner, his figurative virtues, reflected, of course, the mentality of his times. Initially, in the heady days of gold fever, the Forty-niner had represented equal opportunity for all persevering individuals. By the turn of the century, and with the final integration of the former boom town into the nation's urban industrial network, the original features of the miner as city symbol changed in accordance with modified perceptions of economic and social opportunity. In all his depictions, the Forty-niner as symbol of the city by the Bay avoided unchanging virtues. Instead, and based on the changing characteristics of the city, the miner adjusted his expectations in accordance with the contours of his fluid surroundings.

The Forty-niner was never enshrined in bronze in San Francisco during his own lifetime. For that matter, no statues at all adorned the city streets during the boom town era. In a city of private people, each totally engaged in personal economic gain, there appeared to be neither time nor psychological need to produce enduring symbols. As was typical of a boom town mentality, most of those present cared only about filling their coffers swiftly and returning to wherever they had come from. In this milieu of impermanence and functional individuality, enduring works of art never graced the makeshift streets. Only the subsequent need to re-think the limits of economic opportunity after the demise of the gold rush, the growing presence of a permanent population in the late nineteenth century, and the inevitable integration of San Francisco into the continental urban texture, induced the articulation of communal values through elaborate symbols.[9]

Even though no civic statue of the Forty-niner was erected during the gold rush, visual perceptions of the pristine Forty-niner found their way into the city's newspapers and broadsides. Because control of the English language could not be taken for granted, crude sketches and cartoons were a permanent fixture of these publications. These drawings provide a foundation for defining the original contours of the Forty-niner as exemplary hero. A typical image of the Forty-niner emerges from an article published in the local *Hutching's California Magazine* in 1857. (Figure 1) In this magazine, the miner, ordinary looking and solitary, was dressed in sensible clothes. Both hands clutched instruments of toil. Common facial features and hard, but unskilled, work embodied in the miner's grasp of the pick, shovel, and mining pan, suggested that the prospector was by no means of exclusive origin. The California dream, the Forty-niner attested, was accessible to those whose only asset was their labor. The plentiful background of an open range and rushing waters signaled the absence of restraints—economic or social— on the pursuit of happiness, California-style. Individualism, exemplified by the lack of company in suchlike depictions, implied rewards for diligent workers, regardless of the surrounding political or social circumstances. The primary concern of the classic Forty- niner had been easily accessible gold, the class-transcending goal which had catapulted San Francisco from sleepy hamlet into an "instant city." Hence, in his pristine depictions, the classic miner of '49 embodied the aspirations of those who had arrived in the city seeking quick fame and fortune. The iconography of the Forty-niner in gold rush San Francisco implied tangible rewards for just about everybody.

For the purposes of identifying change and continuity in subsequent images of the miner, several fundamental themes in the 1857 magazine sketch should be noted. Technically, the picture may be analyzed from three different perspectives: the relationship between the miner and other human beings, the miner's symbolic ambience represented by the background upon which the miner was placed, and, of course, his vocation, i.e.: the social goals inherent in the figure's attire and tools of his trade. The miner of this early period of urban life in San Francisco

14

stood without any reference to other human figures, be they fellow miners, family members, or other types of settlers in California. The absence of significant others signaled a lack of restraint on the individual desires of the miner. The symbolic background of the miner appeared to be a benign landscape, which, the sluice in the background suggested, could easily be made over to suit the purposes of the fortune seeker. Neither fences nor barriers enclosed this arena of open territory. Indeed, the classical Forty-niner was totally engrossed in an economic pursuit which was far from being exclusive, specialized, or restricted. Personal economic gain appeared to be the only goal of this character. Neither the tools of his trade nor his appearance suggested any ulterior motive. The open range also hinted at the democratic contours of this particular image of the Forty-niner. The surroundings were so vast that they defied individual possession. Somewhere over the mountain range, we are led to suspect, stood another Forty-niner, also preoccupied with a mere sliver of the vast and as yet unappropriated landscape.

This image of the Forty-niner reflected a stage of urban development which Sam Bass Warner has called "privatism." During the initial, boom town stage of San Francisco's development, abundant economic opportunity did away with the need for a guiding hand to distribute the economic cake. Along the east coast, this stage occurred mostly during the colonial period. In San Francisco, perceptions of unlimited opportunity flourished during the first years of the gold-rush, when demand for services that only an urban center could supply focused on the Bay Area. A psychological state of "privatism" existed in which individuals felt that they could pursue personal economic goals without the need for partnerships, long-term planning or extensive economic networking. Three basic conditions confirmed San Francisco's privatism: "its individualized structure of work, its general prosperity, and its open society and economy." San Francisco had all the necessary qualifications for a personalized economic structure: a seemingly insatiable demand for supplies and services resulting from the stream of newcomers to the gold country, the infusion of capital both from outside investment and from local gold revenues, an absence of restraints on individual freedom, and a comparatively small government.[10]

Yet a mere twenty years or so after the initial gold rush, the unregulated market of the boom town era had changed significantly. By the late 1870s, the positivism of the pristine miner seemed outdated and hollow. Harsh economic realities undermined the significance of the workingman prospector as a cultural ideal. Neither patience nor diligence could overcome the multiplying barriers between aspirations and reality in San Francisco. In the closing decades of the nineteenth century, a lull in mining prospects and the increasing impact of railroads had transformed the boom town by the Bay into a large and impersonal commercial center. A network of five eastern routes, all of which had been completed between 1880 and 1890, complemented the original transcontinental line of 1869. Furthermore, the 1887 railroad linkage between San Francisco and Oregon strengthened the city's integration into the transcontinental urban-industrial complex. Indeed, San Francisco became the transportation hub and emporium of the Pacific northwest.[11] At the same time the importance of gold in the California economy had been reduced significantly. Gold yields declined steadily after 1865. By the 1870s, placer mining— which could be carried out with little investment and experience—had all but ceased.[12]

With the streamlining of economic functions came severe social dislocation. The conquest of physical barriers between east and west, north and south, encouraged local manufacturers to control production costs, primarily through the lowering of wages. The bargaining power of those whose skill lay in their labor was diminished further by thousands of hopeful immigrants arriving by railroad. The railroads induced cycles of mass unemployment, which, in turn, intensified social divisions, and produced a general lowering of living standards and economic expectations among working people. "We cannot hope to escape the great law of compensation which exacts some loss for every gain," Henry George had warned in his 1868 prophecy of corporate strangleholds on ordinary people in the modern city.[13] The losses and gains predicted by Henry George were distributed unequally along the lines of economic class. Indeed, the decline of economic opportunity among the unskilled and ordinary working people was accompanied by a rise in the fortunes of prosperous commercial entrepreneurs.

It was during this period of heightened segmentation that the first civic statues appeared in San Francisco's streets. These statues were integral parts of civic uplifting projects imported from the East Coast. Increased standardization of the urbanization process diminished San Francisco's unique qualities while encouraging the duplication of trappings of urban life from cities along the established eastern seaboard. The transplantation of ponderous cultural institutions, such as museums and theaters, and the elevation of the city's appearance through public art projects, accompanied this particular stage of urbanization. In San Francisco grandiose cultural projects were mostly financed by a class of upstarts who had appropriated the reins of economic power in the

16   Signs of Changes

city. These icons of conspicuous culture were monuments to the fortunate few who sought to legitimize their wealth, luck, and business practices. Statues and murals enshrined the personal images of self-defined captains of culture.

A typical example of this trend towards self-aggrandizement materialized in the image of the Forty-niner who appeared quite frequently in the artwork of these civic projects. This first batch of civic representations of the Forty-niner glorified the establishment of a new social system and its priorities. The Forty-niner of civic art departed significantly from the pristine qualities of the workingman-prospector. The classless image of the Forty-niner as an unskilled, individualistic prospector placed in a setting of open land was transformed during the closing decades of the nineteenth century. In accordance with the new order, a dominant caste of flourishing businessmen preached an elitist ethos of survival of the fittest which, they claimed, was an offshoot of California's gold rush mentality.[14] As such, these new pace setters of an urban-industrial complex appropriated the Forty-niner as their own private symbol. Many aspects of the business world were incorporated into the new civic image of the Forty-niner. With growing frequency, statues of the California miner stressed financial acumen, business leadership, and an exclusive background. The ordinary miner had shed his unassuming image and donned, instead, the cloak of the highly skilled entrepreneur.

Douglas Tilden's "Admission Day Fountain," situated in the centrally located intersection of Market and Turk Streets, represented a first step towards identifying entrepreneurship with the California miner. The gift of banker and sometime mayor James D. Phelan, Tilden's 1897 version of the pioneering spirit in the Golden State departed in substance and style from previous conventions. (Figure 2) Few working class people could identify with Tilden's "Native Son." Although his right shoulder supported a symbolic pick, no other signs of labor or tools of trade appeared in the sculpture. The toil-free hands of the miner suggested that the excavation of gold was of ephemeral concern. In addition, the terrain, mountains, and rivers of the gold country were demoted to the extreme lower portion of the pedestal. There, bear skulls entwined with rattlesnakes, represented an esoteric abstract environment which only the initiated could decipher. Instead of the gold country or the paraphernalia of prospecting and manual labor, the allegorical figure of History dominated the backdrop. With the apostle of historical destiny beaming down and with flag in hand, the miner

Ron Robin

appeared to be "stepping forward and shouting" words of guidance to those less fortunate or less talented.[15]

Like previous renditions of the workingman-prospector, Tilden's Forty-niner stood alone. But the element of individualism conveyed in the Native Son's stance suggested new criteria for success in the industrializing city. According to the artist's own description, the miner's symbolic pistol belt set him apart from ordinary people. His weapon identified him with the "virile strength and vigor," of a select group of people.[16] His unique flamboyancy, vigor, and personal sense of mission served as metaphors for the skills of those entrepreneurs who "had built up the industries of the great state and city of the Pacific coast."[17]

As far as the three fundamental elements of comparison are concerned: the miner's symbolic ambience, his relationship with other persons, and his vocation, Tilden's Native Son departed radically from previous visions of the Forty-niner spirit. By associating the miner with the allegorical representation of history rather than with his economic environment or with other mortals, the image underwent a process of mystification. Removing the miner from a recognizable environment posited him as a distant figure, not one who reflected common goals and concerns. The miner was no longer obsessed only with economic pursuit. The grasping of the flag suggested that he was involved in a historical process of progress reserved for the pre-ordained.[18]

While Tilden's fusion of the Forty-niner with businessmen was sheathed in allegorical terms, a contemporaneous statue of San Francisco business leader and successful dentist, Dr. Henry Cogswell, inscribed a similar message in decidedly less subtle tones. In an effort to glorify the contribution of his social class to society, the wealthy dentist thrust upon the city statues of himself as a typical Forty-niner. According to the inscription on the base of Cogswell's most conspicuous statue, the wealthy captain perceived of himself as the prototype of the "Pioneer of 1849," a model product of California's mining days. (Figure 3) Yet, his elegant attire associated him with businessmen rather than prospectors. In fact, nothing pointed towards previous renditions of the Forty-niner and the promise of material rewards for all segments of society. Cogswell was urbane; the classic folk miner, usually depicted in a natural setting, had been an unskilled laborer. Dr. Cogswell was distinguished looking; the miner-workingman had been a plain person. The simple prospector had toiled relentlessly without the promise of definite reward; Cogswell was a professional with well-planned economic goals

18 Signs of Changes

in mind. Dr. Cogswell was a self-styled model for others to follow; the Forty-niner of bygone days had represented the dreams shared by California society at large. Cogswell's statue, like Tilden's Miner, doubled as a drinking fountain. The glass of water in Cogswell's right hand was the ultimate symbol of a paternalistic, elitist temperance spirit.

This temperance motif signalled that the metaphorical content of the statue was directed towards the working-class, whose drinking habits dismayed the likes of Dr. Cogswell. Indeed, the San Francisco of Cogswell's times had about ten saloons for every thousand inhabitants as opposed to a national average of four establishments per thousand inhabitants. Almost every intersection in the city had more than one drinking house, some in the guise of innocent grocery stores, all with private side entrances for discreet patrons.[19] Yet, Cogswell's statue never suggested that the adoption of temperance would allow working people to ascend the pedestal and stand side by side with the doctor. The figure shielded himself from ordinary city folk with elaborate rococo decorations and an aristocratic family coat of arms. This glorification of the Forty-niner as the epitome of an elitist entrepreneurial spirit produced an exemplary hero who was far removed from the grasp of ordinary people. As for the doctor's vocation, nothing in his business suit, his pseudo-classic stance, or detached eye contact suggested connections between the world of the entrepreneur and his target audience. The new industrial order of urban life removed the Forty-niner entrepreneur from the sphere of obtainable goals of working people in San Francisco. He radiated the qualities of pre-ordained leadership and class, rather than egalitarian goals.

Up to this point, then, changing representations of the California miner appears to present a classic case of how the sanctioned "art of any period tends to serve the ideological interests of the ruling class."[20] The mystification of the California miner occurred during a period of what Robert Wiebe has called the segmentation of American urban society.[21] The industrial regime of American cities hardened divisions between those whose only asset was their labor, and their adversaries, those who controlled the means of production. A sense of community which might have transcended economic segmentation was thwarted by the anonymous urban texture. Indeed, many studies of the American city have demonstrated that, even in a relatively fluid environment such as San Francisco, social and economic mobility were quite limited. Although local municipal politics was not always firmly under the control of the entrepreneurial elite, it apparently never relinquished control of the city's economic life.[22]

Ron Robin

However, new editions to the pool of civic representations of the California miner in the early twentieth century challenge the view that municipal art simply glorified the contemporary class structure. Decidedly different images of the Forty-niner also appeared in civic art, even though the patrons of the new images were those same entrepreneurs who had endorsed the previous image of the miner as businessman. In a distinct departure from previous conventions, the new Forty-niner no longer belonged to an exclusive business class; nor did he detach himself, by means of his vocation or origin, from ordinary working people.

The first sign of changing attitudes towards the Forty-niner in civic art appeared in the aftermath of the 1906 earthquake. Even during the initial stages of rehabilitation, when little thought was given to any issue beyond swift reconstruction of the damaged districts, local civic leaders paid uncharacteristic attention to the Cogswell statue; it was removed hastily to the purgatory of the city's storage facility.[23] The banishment of Cogswell's monument was apparently motivated by more than mere distaste for a crude and clumsy work of art. It appears to have had at least some relationship to Cogswell's posing as a Forty-niner, because during this period of rehabilitation, the California miner as businessman had fallen into disrepute.

Glorification of the Forty-niner as businessman did not last for very long. By the turn of the century city people were decidedly skeptical about the applicability of classic individualism in modern city life. Workingmen chafed under the regimentation of a corporate economy rethought their earlier endorsement of unrestrained business practices. They had witnessed callous railroad companies systematically monopolizing the California economy with profit as their only consideration. The railroad "Octopus," the misconceived Golem of entrepreneurial glorification, appeared to have stifled the advantages of a laissez-faire economic environment.[24] Within this context, the Forty-niner, as an individualistic economic man of privileged background, was subject to unfavorable barrages from many segments of San Francisco society.

In assessing the pioneer as businessmen from the perspective of modern city life, the novelist Frank Norris found that these self-appointed cornerstones of society demonstrated a myopic, destructive attitude that overshadowed their virtues.

20

> For all his public spirit, for all his championship of justice and truth, [the Forty-niner] remained the gambler willing to play for colossal stakes ... refusing to wait, to be patient.... [Forty-niners] had no love for the land. They were not attached to the soil. They worked their ranches as a quarter of a century ago they had worked the mines. To get all there was out of the land, to squeeze it dry, to exhaust it seemed their policy. When at last, the land worn out, would refuse to yield, they would invest their money in something else.[25]

San Franciscans lashed out at the pioneer's "love of money, ungodliness and gambling," and at a self-styled aristocracy whose "only distinction consists in the accumulation of large fortunes often obtained by fraud, bribery, and general dishonesty." Only the children of Forty-niners, a prominent clergyman noted in referring to the city's business elite, were worse than their "dyspeptic" fathers.[26]

Recognizing that the Forty-niner's economic and cultural detachment was the main reason for loss of stature, defenders sought resurrection of his credibility by softening the miner's exclusively mercantilistic image. "Love of money is an inherent quality among men in equal distribution in all communities alike," a representative of the Society of California Pioneers reminded critical San Franciscans. The Forty-niner, he suggested, had really been an ordinary type of person beset by commonly shared vices and virtues.[27]

Despite efforts to remodel the features of the Forty-niner as entrepreneur, San Franciscans failed to revive their enthusiasm for the miner as a paragon of privilege. City people by the Bay demanded an image that transcended the triumphs of unusually successful businessmen while addressing the concerns of ordinary citizens. Nevertheless, rejection of the pioneer as businessman did not entail a return to the pioneer as unskilled miner. In rehabilitating the Forty-niner, the California pioneer as gold prospector seemed anachronistic, and as unattractive as that of the aggressive pioneer-businessman. By the turn of the century precious metals and relentless individualism no longer touched the lives of most San Franciscans. Gold leeringly recalled failures and unattainable goals, rather than the promises or solace usually associated with cultural symbols. Individualism, whether in the form of the solitary prospector or the unique businessman, seemed irrelevant in the modern city. Thus, when in the aftermath of the destructive earthquake of 1906, San Franciscans sought relevant symbols to rally around, they rejected both the individualist businessman and the private prospector.

San Francisco's Portola festival in 1909 signalled the trend towards the changing fortunes of the entrepreneur-miner. A mere three years after the earthquake, the city's power wielders decided to celebrate their triumphant rehabilitation of the city with an ambitious municipal festival. Yet, in seeking a figure from the annals of local history who might serve as the central motif for the civic pageant, the organizers attempted to replace the Forty-niner. Instead, they chose Don Gaspar de Portola, Spanish governor of California who had reportedly been the first white man to stumble across San Francisco Bay. Portola fitted the bill because he represented that "proper sort of upstanding and romantic Spanish chap" who was part of an unassuming group of friars and soldiers who chanced upon the Bay during an uncharacteristic lifting of the fog.[28] His main asset was that he belonged to a period far removed from the contentious aspects of contemporary life. Recalling a sylvan period of pre-American rule, he offered a nostalgic trip to a mythological past, rather than a glorification of any particular segment of San Francisco society. Yet, Portola's Hispanic background was apparently too remote for sustained public identification. In fact, he never reached the stage of being enshrined in civic art. Within a few years, Portola was all but forgotten, and the Forty-niner surfaced once again as the central theme of sanctioned art and celebration. Nevertheless, much of the resonant symbolism of Portola was transferred to the new Forty-niner.

The most vivid manifestation of a new and relevant Forty-niner appeared some years after the 1906 earthquake, during the auspicious Panama-Pacific International Exposition of 1915. As a lavishly planned event which caught the attention of the entire nation, the exposition was the logical showcase for contemporary cultural imagery. Through this window into cultural currents of the day, the statues, murals, and paintings at the fair reflected the mood of San Franciscans as they fashioned an approachable folk figure who would distill popular experiences from the uncertainties and realities of a new epoch.

The California miner was a familiar figure at the fair, but he differed significantly from his predecessors. Gold, the principal reason for the state's notoriety, and the staple diet of the Forty-niner-prospector, was transmuted by portraying its glittering qualities as an allegory for California's more mundane characteristics. The Panama-Pacific International Exposition proposed that poppies, wheat, and citrus fruit were the real gilded bounty of twentieth-century California. Those who persisted in the pursuit of unlimited economic gain, such as the businessman-Forty-niner, were castigated. "The Fountain of El Dorado"—a panel designed and executed by sculptor, Gertrude Vanderbilt Whitney —diagnosed the "wealth, power, and fame" inherent in the precious metal as pernicious hallucinations. The scrambling individuals clawing their way to the gateway of El Dorado found the door shut, their strength "expended, their courage gone in the long race for material things."[29]

Signs of individualism and personal gain which had embellished the Forty-niner as businessman were also played down. In general, distinctly American symbols of individualism and solitary action were treated critically at the fairgrounds. The nomadic Indian, a common metaphor for unfettered individualism, was sheathed in a tragic light in James Earl Fraser's "End of the Trail." (Figure 4) Both horse and rider conveyed a sense of finality, the once fearless warrior bowing his head in a gesture of surrender. The Indian's counterpart, represented by Solon Borglum's rendition of the westering pioneer, radiated a similar aura (Figure 5). The wistful gaze of the withdrawn pioneer struck contemporary observers as being hopelessly distant. "With axe and rifle in hand," noted an art critic, "he broods the past." Together with his ancient steed, the patriarch of free spirits appeared to be riding towards oblivion.[30]

Insofar as aggressive individualism appeared in a positive light at the fair, it was presented in a distant, mythological context. Symbols of vigor, daring, and the survival of the fittest adorned arcadian figures associated with ancient history and Greek mythology. On the other hand, a new version of the Forty-niner presented a decidedly sober message.[31] Having discarded the naive fortune-seeking of the pristine prospector as well as the irritating positivism of the businessman-Forty-niner, the miner now provided a more relevant and significant symbolism. His relationship to gold or any other economic pursuit was weakened significantly. In a distinct departure from his individualistic predecessors, the pioneer of '49 at the exposition shared the glories of state building with a large group of contributors to California's past.

One of the exposition's most prominent depictions of the Forty-niner was in the imposing "Nations of the West," a central feature of the exposition's art project. This tribute to the multi-faceted nature of the American experience presented the Forty-niner as a common immigrant, an integral part of a large group. (Figure 6) Placed among a heterogeneous group of participants in the shaping of the frontier experience, the pick-wielding miner appeared as a "German immigrant".[32] Together with a humble Italian laborer, the immigrant miner was featured in the symbolic center of the sculpture. The significance of the miner in this crowded saga was signalled by his location on the right side of the prairie schooner and by the placing of his arm on the lead ox. No other figure in the panel had any physical contact with the symbolic vehicle of the westering nation. Indeed, while most of the flamboyant figures in the panel cast their glances down or sideways, the German miner and his simple Italian peer gazed toward the future. The inherent strength of the miner resulted from his unassuming simplicity, his exemplary ordinary qualities, and his identity as a team member of the westering experience. Here, the miner was demystified by portraying him as a realistic person, an unassuming newcomer from Germany, and by relating his success to the experiences of other participants in the conquering of the American west. Such a transfiguration of the Forty-niner glorified the ordinary, the recognizable, the approachable.

The sociable miner, of foreign origin and placed among a variety of other people, also acknowledged the diversity of his setting. The new Forty-niner as member of a group hinted at a notion of mutual dependence rather than individualism. Removing the miner from the exclusive domain of successful entrepreneurs implied a contemporary awareness of certain limitations on progress and individualism. The re-shaping of the exemplary qualities of the Forty-niner, from individualist to team member, came at a time of a growing acceptance of the limitations of opportunity and mobility in contemporary society. Preference for the sociable-Forty-niner over solitary predecessors suggested a shift in cultural perceptions in accordance with empirical observations. As long as triumphs and good fortune in the American setting were attributed to self-determination and independence, the Forty-niner maintained his individualism and glorified isolation in civic art. Placing the proverbial miner within the context of a group represented a re-orientation of attribution and causality. This pivotal figure of local mythology, who had previously been regarded as an autonomous and independent person, was now seen as a component of the elaborate structure of contemporary American society. The perception of urban life as a coordinated multi-layered matrix introduced significant others to depictions of the Forty-niner.

The "Nations of the West" also hinted at a curious dialectical concept of contemporary society. The westering process, of which the miner was an integral part, was, indeed, a collaborative process. Yet, at the same time, the art piece suggested, even collaborative endeavors could be highly impersonal. With the

24 Signs of Changes

exception of the miner's grasping of the propelling force of progress, neither eye contact nor physical touch linked the central characters of the panel. Like the surrounding urban-industrial context which had produced this statue, each entity in the panel was engaged in a specialized activity which was divorced by time or space, or both from the actions of the other figures. Although the westering experience was a collective enterprise, each character in the panel specialized in one particular aspect of the process.

This collaborative yet impersonal effort served as a central theme in another panel which, once again, placed the miner in the midst of a crowd of co-participants. In Frank DuMond's decorative panel of Pacific coast pioneers welcoming immigrants from the Atlantic seaboard, the miner—clutching pick and shovel—mingled unpretentiously among wheat harvesters and fruit pickers, the "prospectors" of the state's vicarious gold. Only in the distant background, as though belonging to another age, did the indistinct figure of an arcadian gold seeker hack away at barren, uninhabited hills. (Figure 7) The new Forty-niner, on the other hand, shared the land with others; he had no private claim of his own. The Forty-niner's ambience, his relationship with the rest of the world, and his vocation were all radically transformed in Dumond's mural. Of particular importance was the Forty-niner's rapport with fellow toilers. The miner was wedged in at very close quarters with other figures in the mural. In fact, his pick-wielding hand was thrust against the right hand of the farm worker in such a fashion that it was impossible to tell which of the two figures held the pick, and which grasped the sickle. Yet, despite this conscious crowding of figures, the persons represented in the mural seemed unaware of their peers. They all stared forward, with no hint of mutual recognition or overt fraternity.

Crammed quarters and intertwining relationships, counterpoised by impersonal ties, hinted at a new awareness of economic interdependencies that transcended classes. This concept of interdependency, according to historian Thomas Haskell, represented a recognition that in an industrialized society the separate economic activities of vast numbers of people—most of whom would never encounter each other—were intricately linked by unpredictable requirements of supply and demand. Market forces "that had once tended to pry men free from the bonds of traditional society, now reconnected them" in new organizations based on an interconnecting, if impersonal system of production and distribution.[33] Due to interconnecting divisions of labor in the industrial process, and a transportation system which linked urban-industrial centers throughout the United States, action in any one segment of the economy or the country affected all parts of the intertwining capitalist system.

Thus, it appears that the mingling of the miner's hand with the arm of the laborer signalled a recognition that, in a highly industrialized society, no person was autonomous. Interdependence appears to have affected the composition of ambience in the mural, too. Prosperity, represented by the gold of Minerva's shield, was not a direct consequences of the private fortune-seeking activities of the classical miner, who was still depicted in the distant background. Sustained economic abundance depended on a variety of economic enterprises, ranging from a diversified agriculture to a viable transportation network, represented by the protruding oxen and shipping activities in the bay.

The appearance of the Dramatis Personae of this plentiful ambience also signalled another significant feature of the mural. The facial features of the "Pacific Coast Settlers" struck contemporary observers as being almost identical. Similar hair color, indistinct attire, and similar physiological features pointed toward another class-transcending aspect of American urban culture, defined by David Riesman as the move from inner-directed to other-directed consciousness. In an industrial milieu, Riesman noted in his seminal work on *The Lonely Crowd*, Americans abandoned the peculiarities of their inner experiences as guidance, preferring, instead, to emulate the habits and behavior of peers and contemporaries.[34]

Like the consciousness of interdependence, the move towards other-directed modes of urban living produced a common psychological experience, which transcended the reality of hardening economic distinctions, ethnic divisions, and class-related concerns. Even though the cultural content of statues at the exposition was controlled by the business class managers of this enterprise, much of the art work's resonant symbolism avoided a narrow identification with any particular interest group in San Francisco. The iconography of the Forty-niner at the exposition, in "Nations of the West" and "Pacific Coast Settlers," departed from previous civic renditions. The ordinary miner of the Exposition, placed among other people, altered basic perceptions of seeing the world. In contrast to the businessman-miner, whose image was determined by his flamboyant individualism, the sociable-Forty-niner of the exposition focused on the intricate market system of exchange in which all San Franciscans, irrespective of class, were involved. Rather than deriving his success from purely personal qualities, the new Forty-niner utilized perspective to show that he was not the center of the world, but was, rather, one of the cogs in an interconnecting mechanism.

The Forty-niner at the exposition, then, cannot be dismissed as a mere partisan object, the work of a privileged class striving to invent a history to justify its dominant position in society. Nor can one attribute the shifts in the miner's qualities to the peculiarities of his initiators or creators. Patrons of the arts in San Francisco—those who financed civic art and also organized the Panama-Pacific-International Exposition—came from the same, highly selective upper crust. The artists and sculptors were also a monolithic group. With few exceptions, civic artists as well as the craftsmen at the Panama Pacific International exposition belonged to the same professional guilds, had received part of their education in Paris, and were experienced participants in world's fairs and civic uplifting projects.[35]

It remains, then, to be seen whether this "para history" of San Francisco, which shifted emphasis from glorification of autonomous action to an awareness of interdependence, and from an inner-directed to other-directed concept of the self, represents more than a peculiarity of public art of mainstream San Francisco. In fact, local politics—the most sensitive indicator of popular attitudes—appears to validate the significance of visual representations of civic art. In their crowning of political heroes at the municipal level, San Franciscans also moved from admiration for the businessman-pioneer toward support for a sociable, somewhat generic folk figure as quintessence of the Forty-niner spirit.

From 1880 and until 1901, during the heyday of the Forty-niner as entrepreneur in civic art, city people by the Bay elected accomplished businessmen to the city's highest and most visible office.[36] The most conspicuous of San Francisco's entrepreneurial mayors was James D. Phelan, mayor from 1897 to 1901, and donor of the business-oriented statue of the miner on Market and Turk streets. In addition to the lip service that he paid to popular anti-Chinese sentiment, Phelan's appeal was linked to his bid to implement his business acumen in the municipal sphere. The basic thrust of his proposals—municipal ownership of city utilities and institutionalization of the mayor as the city's sole executive authority—promised to dissolve the corrupt nexus between politicians and economic interests. Under the old city charter of 1856, both executive and legislative functions had resided in a bribe-ridden board of supervisors. The reform document transferred all administrative and legislative functions to the city's chief elected official and his technocratic appointees. The superimposing of a "systematic, rational, consistent" and business-like system upon the city, Phelan advocated, would produce an honest, and impartial municipal apparatus.[37]

Phelan mistook popular support of municipal reform for deference. His high-handed manner of running the city and a reluctance to acknowledge diversity in an intensely political city led to a temporary setback in his political career and the ultimate decline of San Francisco's businessmen-mayors. Phelan's political fortunes received their first major blow in the winter of 1901, when he handled a bubonic plague crisis as chairman of the board dealing with cost-cutting measures rather than as a politician in an intensely political city.[38] In an effort to eradicate the plague in a professional and businesslike fashion, whole neighborhoods were cordoned off and interstate commerce was limited at the solitary discretion of city health officials. Despite the crippling effect of these municipal measures on the city's economy, Phelan's administration ruled out any form of consultation with the various political factions affected by the crisis.

San Franciscans of all political colors responded unfavorably to these trappings of corporate practices. Both businessmen and supporters of labor vented their dissatisfaction with the mayor by ridiculing the mismatch between Phelan's pretentious handling of the crisis and his diminutive stature. Irrespective of their other differences, a broad spectrum of local politicians warned that the city's ruin would be brought about by insensitive technocrats rather than disease.[39] Phelan, as reflected in his Native Sons' Monument and his concept of politics, associated leadership with the principles of business administration. His constituents, however, likened his attitudes to despotism.

A year after the epidemic, the great San Francisco general strike of 1901 sealed Phelan's fate. The strike, which began as a dispute between draying companies and teamsters, rapidly spread throughout the city. Tense relations between labor unions and employment associations had been festering for some time. Consequently, both sides pounced upon the opportunity of an isolated incident between teamsters and drayers to flex muscles and contain opponents. Phelan, to the dismay of labor and business, approached the strike as a detached technocrat rather than as a partisan. He intended to keep the urban machine moving at all costs and irrespective of the political conflict at hand. His impartiality—protection of strikebreakers balanced by an unwillingness to unleash the police at the bid of business leaders—merely annoyed both sides.[40]

28   Signs of Changes

Implementing the tidy, impersonal features of cost-benefit analysis in the municipal sphere bothered San Franciscans. His preference for administrative efficiency over the bartering of political factions did not inspire affection in Phelan's fellow citizens. The impersonal forces of industrialization and urbanization strengthened perceptions of politics as a beleaguered but valid bastion of control over personal destiny. Neither employers nor workingmen were prepared to defer to the dispassionate policies of a would-be corporate executive.

The contrast between Phelan and his accommodating successors bore a striking resemblance to the differences between statues of the businessman-pioneer and those of the sociable Forty-niner. Phelan's efficiency-oriented administration was followed by the free-wheeling Union Labor Party, led by "Boss" Abraham Ruef and dapper mayor Eugene Schmitz. Despite its militant-sounding name, the Union Labor party did not derive its strength from an exclusive courting of the blue collar vote. The party merely sought equitable division of the municipal pork-barrel among a variety of city people, including businessmen and workers. Boss Ruef commanded no intricate political machine, nor did he enjoy grass roots support in the city's working-class neighborhoods.

Neither automatic ballot stuffing nor corrupt office seekers propelled this party of spoil seekers into power. Political success was the brainchild of Boss Ruef and his marketing of attractive politicians of the people. Longevity within the political arena, Ruef had surmised, depended upon appealing to the city's diverse social and cultural fiber but without annoying anyone. Consequently, Ruef's designs hinged upon a candidate for mayor who would appeal to a broad, seemingly incompatible coalition of warring economic factions and mutually suspicious ethnic wards. His choice, Eugene Schmitz, was ideal.[41]

Born in San Francisco, Mayor Eugene Schmitz boasted both Irish and German ancestry. In a polyglot city of 345,000 citizens in which over a 100,000 had at least one German parent, and another 95,000 were of Irish descent, Schmitz's blood ties proved indispensable. His mild brand of Catholicism elicited additional support from 115,000 co-religionists. Connections with labor unions through his leadership of the innocuous musician's union gained him further support without alienating business interests. In fact, he was somewhat of a small businessman himself, while, as a musician, he commanded the respect of men of culture. Tall and handsome, affable, and a model family man, Schmitz represented the much-coveted common denominator, not unlike the new image of the ordinary Forty-niner in civic art.

Unheralded disaster eventually toppled the Union Labor party. A weak party organization, unscrupulous office holders, and the misguided choice of a crusading district attorney terminated the reign of Schmitz and Ruef. In a spectacular series of graft trials, Schmitz lost his tenure and Ruef, almost five years of his freedom. Nevertheless, their downfall did not spark changes in attitudes towards politics among San Franciscans. After a brief interregnum of class-oriented municipal struggles, the election of James Rolph in 1911 sustained the tradition of politics as an arena for accommodation and broad public consensus.

In defeating incumbent mayor Patrick McCarthy, who had transformed the amiable Union Labor party into a class-conscious action group, "Sunny Jim" brought together an extraordinary coalition of mainstream Democrats and Republicans, workingmen, and non-partisan middle-class voters.[42] Ostensibly a Republican, Rolph's success did not derive from partisan posturing. In fact, he garnered support by avoiding controversial issues and declarations of personal convictions. He refrained from comment on the graft prosecution against Abraham Ruef and Eugene Schmitz and, before his own election to California's highest office, he never endorsed candidates for the state's heated gubernatorial races.

Beaming "endearingly democratic mannerisms," this self-made millionaire continuously stressed his ties with common citizens by residing throughout his career in the blue-collar Mission district where he had been born.[43] Rolph's emphasis on the unavoidable ties among city people, irrespective of class or stature, hampered attempts to revive doctrinal politics at the municipal level. Even Samuel Gompers—the charismatic leader of the American labor movement—failed to persuade supporters of labor in San Francisco to "elect faithful workingmen with union cards in their pockets."[44]

Rolph ruled San Francisco triumphantly for nineteen years, his genial nature a reflection of public desire for simple and comprehensible virtues. "Sunny Jim's" undisputed tenure proved that the majority of city people desired leaders who were a "good mixture" who pursued the line of common interests of an eclectic constituency.[45] As a political version of the interdependent Forty-niner, Rolph acknowledged the demise of individualism and sought accommodation with San Francisco's diverse populace. As such, he contrasted sharply with his predecessors, the businessmen-pioneers of impeccable background and unique talent who had ruled the roost before him. Rolph's departure from the visions of his predecessors reflected changes in popular paragons of virtue. "Sunny Jim's" political millings with city people of all persuasions, like the iconography of the sociable Forty-niner, reassured San Franciscans of a common human condition shared by all urbanites.

From workingman-prospector, through Forty-niner-businessman, and finally to the sociable miner who was neither better nor worse than other ordinary people, the miner's changing image in San Francisco's civic art demonstrated the fluidity of urban culture. When contemporary mores lost their relevance in a swiftly-moving environment, San Franciscans, as typical city people, expediently remodeled their symbols of culture.

It remains, now, to be seen, to what degree did this pragmatic concept of American culture, permeating the public and political symbols of mainstream society, affect the lives of ordinary people in San Francisco, in particular those who subscribed to the various sub-cultures of this American city. San Francisco was a vast mosaic of ethnic groups, some of which were tolerated, other were considered pariahs. Race, color, and economic competition accounted in no small part for the variety of reactions towards immigrants. Yet in the case of San Francisco these traditional benchmarks for seeking American reactions to newcomers do not provide a satisfactory answer for understanding the extraordinary lenient attitudes towards newcomers from eastern Europe and the Mediterranean basin.

In other American cities Jews and Italian were frequently "accused" of being as racially divergent as Asians; their presence often posed a direct economic threat to established groups, too. Nevertheless, in San Francisco they never aroused the vicious animosities which were heaped upon citizens of color. The following chapters seeks the answer in the local version of Jewish and Italian sub-cultures which mirrored much of the pliable cultural guidelines of mainstream society. Much like the myths of San Francisco's established elites, these two groups of immigrants developed a "para-history" which focused upon the manipulation of modified versions of their particular myths and traditions in order to enhance adaptation during a period of swiftly changing realities.

This pliable attitude towards their own cultures was made possible by a variety of fortuitous circumstances, cultural and political. The jostling of political forces, racial prejudices, and preconceptions of classical Italian and Hebraic

Ron Robin 31

cultures furnished a positive background for the activities of Italians and Jews in San Francisco, and encouraged the transformation of foreign cultures to uniquely American circumstances. It is to these aspects that we now turn our attention.

Figure 1
The Forty-niner as Simple Prospector.
From *Hutching's California Magazine*, 1857.
(Courtesy, Bancroft Library, University of California).

Figure 2
The Forty-niner departs from Singular Mining Concerns.
Native Sons' Monument, San Francisco, 1897.
(Photograph by the Author).

Figure 3
The Forty-niner as Businessman.
Henry Cogswell Statue, San Francisco, Circa 1900.
(Courtesy, Bancroft Library, University of California).

Figure 4
Disillusion with Individualism.
James Earl Fraser, "End of the Trail."
Panama-Pacific Exposition, San Francisco, 1915.
(Courtesy, Bancroft Library, University of California).

Figure 5
Individualism as Anachronism.
Solon Borglum, "The Pioneer."
Panama-Pacific Exposition, San Francisco, 1915.
(Courtesy, Bancroft Library, University of California).

Figure 6
The Forty-niner as Ordinary Immigrant.
A. Sterling Calder, Frederick Roth, Leo Lentilli,
"Nations of the West."
Panama-Pacific Exposition, San Francisco, 1915.
(Courtesy, Bancroft Library, University of California).

Figure 7
The Interdependent Forty-niner.
Frank Dumond, "Pacific Coast Settlers."
Panama-Pacific Exposition, San Francisco, 1915.
(Courtesy, Bancroft Library, University of California).

Notes

1. Amy Bernardy, *America Visutta* (Torino, 1911), 221-234.
2. Daniel J. Boorstin, *The Americans; The National Experience* (New York, 1965) 275-324, discusses the peculiarities of American grammar.
3. Census figures cited in Gunther Barth, *Instant Cities* (New York, 1975), 135.
4. J. B. Jackson, " The Vernacular City, " in Larry P. Fuller (ed.), *The Land, the City, and the Human Spirit* (Austin, Texas, 1985), 48-61.
5. Frederick S. Lamb, "Municipal Art," *Municipal Affairs*, 1 (December, 1897), 674-688; Karl Bitter, "Municipal Sculpture," *ibid.*, 2 (March 1898), 74; H. K. Bush-Brown, "New York City Monuments," *ibid.*, 3 (December, 1899), 602-615; Charles Lopez, "Municipal Sculpture," *ibid.*, 5 (June 1901), 696-708; Elma Graves, "Municipal Art," *American Journal of Sociology*, 6 (June 1900-May 1901), 673-681.
6. For a survey of mostly political civic art in American cities at the turn of the century see: J. Sanford Saltus and Walter Tisne', *Statues of New York* (New York, 1923); James Goode, *The Outdoor Sculpture of Washington, D. C.* (Washington, D. C., 1974); Dennis Nawrachi, *Art in Detroit Public Places* (Detroit, 1980); Ira Bach and Mary Gray, *A Guide to Chicago's Public Sculpture* (Chicago, 1983); Vernon Gay and Marilyn Evert, *Discovering Pittsburgh's Sculpture* (Pittsburgh, 1983). On the need to produce civic art which would reflect the concerns of ordinary people see: "Public Art in American Cities," *Municipal Affairs*, 2 (March, 1898), 1-13.
7. Michael Grant, *Roman Myths* (London, 1971), introduction.
8. Horatio Alger, *The Young Miner; or Tom Nelson in California* (New York, 1879), 6.
9. On the creation of a permanent sense of civic awareness in San Francisco see Gunther Barth, *Instant Cities; Urbanization and the Rise of San Francisco and Denver* (New York, 1975), 128-228.
10. Sam Bass Warner Jr., *The Private City* (Philadelphia, 1968), 3-21. The boom town era of San Francisco is described in Roger Lotchin, *San Francisco, 1846-1856; From Hamlet to City* (New York, 1965).
11. Robert Riegel, *The Story of Western Railroads* (Lincoln, Nebraska, 1963), 179-211.
12. Ira Cross, *History of the Labor Movement in California* (Berkeley, 1935), 61-64.

40 Signs of Changes

13. Henry George, "What the Railroad Will Bring Us," *Overland Monthly*, 1 (October, 1868), 287.
14. Peter R. Decker, *Fortunes and Failures; White Collar Mobility in Nineteenth Century San Francisco* (Cambridge, Mass., 1978), 231-249.
15. *Ibid.*
16. Douglas Tilden, "Description of "Admission Day Fountain," in San Francisco Board of Superisors, *Municipal Reports, 1896-1897* (San Francisco, 1897), appendix, 392. The monument is also referred to alternately as the "Native Sons' Monument."
17. "Description of H. T. Holmes," *Historical Review of Industries of San Francisco* (San Francisco, 1887), 139. This publication, which can be found in the Bancroft Library, identifies most of the city's business leaders with the so-called Forty-niner spirit and age.
18. Another rendition of the Forty-niner, which also played upon this notion of a pre-ordained miner participating in a monumental historical process, appeared in the James Lick Pioneer Monument (1894). The monument still stands at the intersection of Grove, Hyde, and Market streets in San Francisco.
19. United States Bureau of the Census, *Report on the Social Statistics of Cities in the United States at the Eleventh Census, 1890* (Washington, D. C., 1892), 108-117, table 71; Benjamin E. Lloyd, *Lights and Shades in San Francisco* (San Francisco, 1876), 182-185. On the working class and alcohol in turn-of the-century San Francisco see Jack London, *John Barleycorn* (Santa Cruz, Ca., New Edition, 1981).
20. John Berger, *Ways of Seeing* (London, 1972), 86.
21. Robert Wiebe, *The Segmented Society* (New York, 1975).
22. Peter Decker, *Fortunes and Failures; White Collar Mobility in Nineteenth Century San Francisco* (Cambridge, Mass., 1978) discusses social mobility in American cities in general and the particular San Francisco context. The political fortunes of various economic interests in San Francisco are analyzed in Walton Bean, *Boss Ruef's San Francisco* (Berkeley, 1972). See also James P. Walsh, "Abe Ruef Was Not a Boss; Machine Politics, Reform, and San Francisco," *California Historical Quarterly*, 51 (Spring, 1972), 3-17 and Spencer Olin Jr., *California Politics, 1846-1920; The Emerging Corporate State* (San Francisco, 1981).
23. Martin Nathan, "San Francisco's Fin de Siècle Bohemian Renaissance."

Ron Robin

24. George Mowry, *The California Progressives* (Berkeley, 1951) analyzes both the background and political legacy of California's reform-minded business class.

25. Frank Norris, *The Octopus; a Story of California* (New York, 1906), 298. A similar portrayal of the Forty-niner appears in Jack London, *Valley of the Moon* (Santa Cruz, Ca., New Edition, 1981), 413-14.

26. San Francisco *Chronicle*, January 29, 1894, 3; "Address by Outgoing Mayor Adolph Sutro," *Municipal Reports, 1894-1895*, appendix, 9. A synopsis of attacks on the businessman-Forty-niner appears in "Dedication of the James Lick Monument," *Municipal Reports, 1893-1894*, 252-257.

27. "Dedication of the James Lick Monument."

28. The history of the Portola festival is described briefly in Frank M. Todd, *The Story of the Exposition*, 5 vols. (New York, 1921), i, 43-46.

29. Juliet James, *Sculpture of the Exposition* (San Francisco, 1915)

30. George Perry, *The Sculpture and Mural Decorations of the Exposition* (San Francisco, 1915), 34.

31. Examples of the foreign context of social-Darwinism messages are "Fountain of Energy" and "The Survival of the Fittest" in James, *Sculpture of the Exposition*, 3, 66. A different interpretation of the sculptures at the Exposition is discussed in Elizabeth N. Armstrong, "Hercules and the Muses; Public Art and the Fair," in Burton Benedict, *The Anthropology of World's Fairs; San Francisco's Panama-Pacific Exposition of 1915* (Berkeley, 1983)

32. Eugene Neuhaus, *The Art of the Exposition* (San Francisco,1915), 36.

33. Thomas L. Haskell, *The Emergence of Professional Social Science; The American Social Science Association and the Nineteenth Century Crisis of Authority* (Urbana, Illinois, 1977), 24-47.

34. David Riesman, *The Lonely Crowd; a Study of the Changing American Character* (Revised Edition, Garden City, N. Y., 1953).

35. Biographies of the artists at the exposition appear in John Trusk and J. Nilsen Lauvrick, *Catalogue De Luxe of the Department of Fine Arts, Panama Pacific Exposition* (San Francisco, 1915).

36. William A. Bullough, *The Blind Boss and His City; Christopher Augustine Buckley and Nineteenth Century San Francisco* (Berkeley, 1979), 120 discusses the election of businessmen mayors from 1879 until the end of the century.

37. James Phelan, *Municipal Conditions and the New Charter* (San Francisco, 1896), 4, 6, 79.

42 Signs of Changes

38. Philip A. Kalisch, "The Black Death in Chinatown; Plague and Politics in San Francisco, 1900-1914," *Arizona and the West*, 14 (Summer, 1972), 113-136.

39. San Francisco *Call*, March 10, 1900, 12; March 13, 1900, 5. San Francisco *Chronicle*, March 10, 1900, 7; March 25, 1900, 20.

40. Cross, *History of California Labor*, 12-21; Robert E. L. Knight, *Industrial Relations in the San Francisco Bay Area, 1900-1918* (Berkeley, 1960), 39-95.

41. The chronicles of the Union Labor Party are documented in Walton Bean, *Boss Ruef's San Francisco* (Berkeley, 1972). See also James P. Walsh, "Abe Ruef Was Not a Boss; Machine Politics, Reform, and San Francisco," *California Historical Quarterly*, 51 (Spring, 1972), 3-17.

42. On James Rolph's career see Moses Rischin, "Sunny Jim Rolph, the First Mayor of all the People," *California Historical Quarterly*, 53 (Summer, 1974), 165-172; David W. Taylor, *The Life of James Rolph Jr.*, (San Francisco, 1934), 1-7.

43. Herman Goldbeck, "The Political Career of James Rolph Jr." (M.A. University of California, Berkeley, 1936), 4-12, 160.

44. San Francisco *Labor Clarion*, September 8, 1911, 3-5.

45. Interview with William Bauer, "Growing Up in Cities" (Ms. Bancroft Library, University of California, 1970).

CHAPTER 2
SAN FRANCISCO SMELTING POT

Groping for an evocative description of life in cosmopolitan San Francisco, Robert Louis Stevenson coined a subtle departure from a much-worn phrase. The city, he mused, resembled a "smelting pot."[1] Stevenson's analogy for the extraction of pure, fundamental elements from foreign substances rather than the indiscriminate fusion of cultures associated with the melting pot, hinted at the tolerant, albeit qualified, acceptance of newcomers in San Francisco. If skin color or radically divergent heritages did not remove them from the pale of American San Francisco, immigrants could slip into pre-existing cultural frameworks.

From its inception as a city, diversity had been the mainstay of life in San Francisco. While most western states "had been peopled by a steady influx of settlers from two or three older states," observed James Bryce, "California was settled by a sudden rush of adventurers from all parts of the world."[2] The 1890 census indicated that San Francisco had the largest proportion of foreign-born residents among the thirty-five principal cities in the United States. From a total population of 229,000 almost 127,000—more than forty-two percent—were foreign born. The imminent opening of the Panama Canal suggested to many that the unabated flow of newcomers would probably persist.[3]

Heterogeneity also existed among American-born residents of the city. Almost every state in the Union was represented in the Bay Area, thereby accentuating the need for common frames of reference for both restless Americans and uprooted immigrants.[4] For better or for worse, it seemed that California had been "providentially held in reserve for the permanent settlement of Fin de Siecle migrants of this and other lands."[5]

Seeking to rationalize the inevitable presence of strangers, San Franciscans accepted newcomers as a nexus between past disillusions brought on by the demise of their gold rush boomtown and aspirations for positive progress through manageable industrialization. In both popular thought and public policy, the immigrant experience provided the building blocks for reconciling a free-for-all gold rush mentality with the discipline of the factory. As such, the immigrant psyche was expected to be sufficiently malleable to accommodate all social and economic classes. Working people singled out moral fiber and class loyalty among newcomers; others discerned the prized qualities of perseverance and

44 Signs of Changes

industriousness sought by entrepreneurs. Contradictory images of immigrants enhanced their acceptability, because anyone, regardless of political orientation and social status, could create a hero after his or her own ideas. Flexible concepts of newcomers counterpoised economic strife, ethnic tensions, and social conflict in the polyglot city.

Accepting the presence of foreigners was also a pragmatic matter for San Francisco. Mathematical assessments of immigrant impact at the polls hastened favorable attention from the entire political spectrum. Political realism and popular myth eventually translated into public policy when, in 1914, Californians established a San Francisco-based state agency for the purpose of addressing the needs of foreign-born residents. The San Francisco context of a mobile society seeking self approval through the presence of newcomers represented a particularly interesting case because it flourished simultaneously with an onslaught of aggressive anti-immigration movements.

In 1882, a federal law curtailing the immigration of Chinese laborers culminated a protracted struggle which had seen the first salvo fired in San Francisco's anti-Chinese "Sandlot Riots" of July 1877.[6] Exclusion of Japanese immigrants through a series of "Gentlemen's Agreements" found its most powerful base in San Francisco, too.[7] The California legislature, in barring state employment of non-citizens, European and Asians, furnished another tool for restricting immigration through control of the market place. The city of San Francisco employed a similar policy by limiting the access of non-citizens to the municipal pork barrel.[8]

Animosity towards immigrants in California did not derive from Xenophobia, the fear of foreigners per se. Multi-national Californians had no firm native heritage to justify their opposition to the influx of newcomers. By and large, discrimination was aimed at those whose physical appearance belied the immigrant mystique. People of color, both newcomers and native born, could not span the chasm between cherished traditions and expectations. The immigrant as symbol—an independent-minded individual who adapted to the continuing march of change inherent in the American landscape, without eroding the stature of peers and fellow strugglers—needed to look like the inventors of the myth. The idealized immigrant had flexible virtues. But, in accordance with the onus of American culture, the civilizing of the continent was synonymous with the European complexion of its conquerors.[9]

Hence, physiognomy, the art of discovering human qualities through outward appearances, was considered the principal guide to character.[10] Radically foreign features contradicted contemporary images of the pioneering spirit. Accordingly, economic phobias and social fears were phrased in the language of an alien conspiracy of strange looking people against a white American way of life. "While we are going to the Philippines to assimilate the natives there," a speaker at an anti-Asian rally in San Francisco observed, "the Japanese and Chinese are coming here to assimilate us."[11] Great emphasis was placed on the physical appearance of Asians who, even when they attempted to adopt American mannerisms, were not accepted by whites.[12] Asian features were synonymous with "insidious and unfair competition" and the erosion of an American "competition with nature in new lands."[13] The stereotyping of Chinese and Japanese in California linked skin color to destructive migratory habits and disdain for stability.[14]

Similar obstacles confronted blacks, American by birth but alien by color. In popular images—cartoons, comic strips, and the stage—the stereotyping of woolly hair, pitch black faces, and animal-like thick lips cast a mask of inferiority over blacks thereby denying them any sense of individuality. A familiar figure on the vaudeville stage in San Francisco, the overdressed, shiftless urban black who clumsily aped white mannerisms was a creature of impulses, often intoxicated, always ludicrously inferior by virtue of his skin color.[15] Even from the venerable halls of the University of California, a professor of history identified the physical features of Afro-Americans with their incompatibility with American ways. Although blacks often emulated American mannerisms, Professor Bernard Moses stated emphatically, they could not shed the burden of "wild barbarism" associated with contemporary concepts of color.[16] In this sense blacks resembled California's Mexican population. They, too, seemed "to have a specific gravity which keeps them at the bottom of the ... melting pot," noted a social worker, the reason being that they were more like peonic non-white Indians than Spanish conquerors.[17]

The arbitrary linkage between distinct physical appearances and American mores had immediate ramifications in the market place. For the most part, local employers preferred foreign-born immigrants over the hiring of blacks, even though European newcomers were less familiar with local ways than their Afro-American counterparts. Economic legislation almost always contained clauses excluding Asians from its benefits.[18]

46 Signs of Changes

Unlike San Francisco's citizens of color who were denied the full benefits of modern city life, the preferred status of European immigrants was rationalized by fabricating a pantheon of California heroes whose deeds warranted the ensuing privileges heaped upon their compatriots. Center stage was occupied by veteran immigrants whose presence in San Francisco could be traced to the beginnings of statehood. Adolph Gustav Ross, a German immigrant who had made his fortune through astute real estate dealings in the Bay Area in 1847 was considered typical of the "best among our pioneers."[19] Intelligence, personal simplicity, moral fortitude, and business acumen were among the enumerated qualities from which both he and his adopted state had benefited.

Germans, like all other immigrant groups who met the criteria of the ideal immigrant, furthered their claims of privilege by creating fortuitous interventions of their brethren in pivotal events in the history of California. Thus, local Germans claimed that a German Jesuit in Baja California had been the first European to urge settlement in Alta California. The first major explorer of California, according to local German lore, had been a German too. John Sutter, successful miner and businessman, and leader of the challenge to Mexican sovereignty in California, was usurped by local Germans who chose to ignore his Swiss origins. The ill-fated Donner party, the 1849 immigrant train trapped in the snow-bound Sierras and "symbol of the sufferings and hardships of early immigrants," was purportedly comprised of Germans, too.[20]

Within this context of ethnic privilege and economic disparities, society exhibited a surprisingly lenient attitude towards certain immigrant groups, particularly those from eastern Europe and the Mediterranean basin.[21] To be sure, southern and eastern European immigrants frequently appeared as racially and culturally divergent as Asian or Hispanics. Their presence often posed a direct economic threat to established groups, too.[22] Nevertheless, European immigrants never aroused the vicious animosities heaped upon citizens of color.

In part, this may be attributed to political pragmatism. Most European newcomers settled in the state's burgeoning cities where large concentrations of voters could make or break any political career. According to the census of 1910, fifty-six percent of the state's population huddled in cities of over five thousand, up from approximately forty percent in 1880. Californians also witnessed a continuous rise in the population density in their cities of over ten thousand—from twenty-seven percent in 1880, to over thirty-seven percent of the state's entire population in 1910. In San Francisco, the largest city in the state, foreign born and second generation European immigrants outnumbered those of native parentage by almost 3 to 1. With estimates of impending immigration from Europe to California through the soon to be completed Panama. Canal running as high as four thousand newcomers per month, political interest groups from a broad spectrum of society actively solicited immigrant votes in San Francisco.[23]

No less important than the expediency of politics were the much noted physiological similarities between California and certain European landscapes. San Francisco, often portrayed as a transplanted European city, was part and parcel of the ongoing search for acceptable forms of historical continuity in a rootless climate. The legitimization of historical antecedents in California was a major preoccupation among San Franciscans. The city's economic elite, most threatened by lack of solid legitimacy in economically perilous San Francisco, energetically cultivated both real and contrived ties between themselves and the Republic's revolutionary progenitors. The Sons of the American Revolution Society, one of the nation's premier genealogical societies, had originated in California, where lack of common ancestry accentuated the need for a re-writing of shared historical origins.[24]

In the long run, the fabrication of entrenched aristocracies did not sit well in an urban setting of fluctuating fortunes.[25] For those who sought broader based myths of common roots, a vague Hispanic heritage provided a more comfortable source for historical pillaging. By virtue of the city's diverse population, few claimed privilege through direct links to the Californios. Rather than blood lines, it was the Hispanic ambience that had brought San Franciscans together. "I am a Californian," declared a heroine in a popular historical romance of the time. "Even if I haven't Spanish blood in my veins," she noted, carefully distinguishing between Spanish culture and its less attractive non white Mexican offspring, "I have the spirit of the old Padres."[26]

The ever-growing presence of European immigrants in the city encouraged the synthesizing of historical roots beyond a narrow Hispanic environment and towards a broader European context. A distinct European presence in San Francisco rebuffed the typical Eastern snubbing of the Instant City by the Bay. Exotic corners, such as the city's Latin Quarter, radiated an attractive "flavor of the foreigner," reminiscent of the opera and other revered cultural institutions of European origin. European traditions of long standing projected a semblance of security in volatile San Francisco. Superimposing stable foreign elements on the city enhanced San Franciscans' sense of permanence. At the same time, these

48 Signs of Changes

foreign attributes were tempered by uniquely American, "Rooseveltian Qualities" of enterprise and astute common sense associated with the popular personality of President Theodore Roosevelt.[27] In combining American characteristics with respectable European traits, southern European culture claimed legitimacy, especially as it adapted admirably to the Bay Area's geographical characteristics.

If physiographical similarities existed, the physiogenical attributes of European immigrants could be easily metabolized and expropriated. American man on the Pacific shore, when tempered by the quasi-Mediterranean features of the region, would inevitably become the highest product of modern civilization, noted an enthusiastic scientist.[28] In contrast to the typical physiogenical proclamation that changes in "bodily forms" would radically make over European neophytes in America, San Franciscans fostered a converse legend. As part of the search for a usable heritage they accepted the immigrant as physical prototype of the ideal Californian.[29]

Citizens of culture were quick to point out their state's topographical similarities with Greece, birthplace of Western concepts of art and philosophy, with Italy, where modern doctrines of law and societal organization had originated, and with Palestine, the source of Judeo-Christian religions. These analogies were particularly visible in San Francisco's tourist brochures:

> Here is the soft air and blue sky of Milan, the marine outlook of Naples, with Mount Tamalpais impersonating Vesuvius, the hills of Rome, the winter climate of the Riviera, and people the combination of New England energy and oriental luxury....Not only is the area of the state in latitudes corresponding to the Holy Land, but the characteristics of climate, soil, and flora, as well as the products of agriculture and horticulture are similar to that corner of the earth where was once the Promised Land.[30]

The emphasis on California as a synthetic version of Italy and ancient Palestine reflected the inordinate attention paid to Jews and Italians in San Francisco, the largest groups of urban newcomers at the turn of the century. With approximately thirty thousand members each by 1915, these two communities had exceeded numerically the older foreign born Irish and German elements, and their proportions were expected to rise continuously. Not surprisingly, a policy of accommodation towards these two "outstanding immigrant groups in San Francisco" decorated most political banners, from Labor to conservative business platforms.[31]

In the municipal school system, a trusty barometer of political accommodation, Jews and Italians garnered numerous concessions. The Board of Education honored Jewish protests by replacing readings of the *Merchant of Venice* with *Julius Caesar* in the city's high schools. At the same time, the school board encouraged Italian language instruction in the predominately Italian North Beach district.[32] Even outspoken critics of ethnocentricity , such as the San Francisco Call, deemed it politically expedient to support this policy. "The knowledge of another language helps us understand our own," an editorial noted, piously quoting the German poet Goethe that "he who knows but one language knows none."[33]

Political pragmatism also inspired organized labor in San Francisco to develop a reluctant, but positive stand on immigrants. Anti-immigrant sentiment, when expressed by local unions, focused primarily on Asians. Restrictions on immigration from Europe through devices such as literacy tests were approached with much trepidation for fear of alienating potential recruits.[34] Even William McCarthy, a trade union leader of the nativist persuasion, demonstrated that political acumen could override prejudices and economic fears. He actively courted immigrants by publishing foreign language propaganda in his 1910 bid for the office of mayor of San Francisco.[35]

Beyond the political wisdom involved in embracing San Francisco's two largest immigrant groups, Jews and Italians also fulfilled the important function of matching the stereotypical expectations of existing beliefs. Italians, in particular, appeared to have captured the flexible spirit of the immigrant mystique: a person who was both resolute and compassionate, hardened individualist and class-conscious union member, humble farmer and flamboyant entrepreneur

Common knowledge held that the Italian colony in San Francisco, "this typical colony of Altruria in our midst," had derived its values from an idyllic Europe which had nourished the American republic and nurtured California during its formative years. As proud tillers of the soil, according to the typical observation, they brought with them notions of self-help and perseverance associated with the American creed.[36]

Friends of labor were particularly struck by worker solidarity among Italians. A case in point was the Italian Bakers' Union which refused to relinquish

50 Signs of Changes

a rule requiring its members to offer their jobs to unemployed union members for four days a month. Citing concern for the families of their unemployed members, the Italian bakers resisted their employers to the point of resigning en masse and forming their own bakers' cooperative.[37] When labor unrest at the turn of the century convinced union members of the necessity to recruit members from the dominant immigrant groups, Italians constituted a primary target of this drive. Because their numbers were great and because they appeared to share the concern of native-born working people, labor unions contemplated the potential gains of immigrant support.[38]

Sensing no apparent contradiction, San Francisco's economic elite endorsed the positive attitude of Labor towards Italians. "He raises families and establishes homes, he sends his children to schools to be educated," noted the pro-business journal, *The Wasp*, alluding to the modicum of stability that these qualities introduced into a restless industrial proletariat. At the same time, an abundant supply of industrious Italian workers provided entrepreneurs with a more attractive pool of labor than the uncomfortably distant Asian.[39] Despite their humble backgrounds, an organ of Big Business assured, Italians differed from Asiatics in their acceptance of the American creed of progress. Their fundamental qualities practically guaranteed that within a short period they would achieve the status of home owners, perhaps even develop into aspiring capitalists.[40]

Of course, not all San Franciscans relished the presence of Italians. Mary Roberts Coolidge, a champion of the Chinese in California, protested that despite their caucasian appearance, San Francisco's Italians should not be idealized. Drunkenness, pathologically violent behavior, and lack of cleanliness were part of life in the city's Italian quarter, she claimed. As such, Italians were more like the antithesis of the ideal immigrant—the supposedly inassimilable, clannish oriental—than San Francisco's paragons of virtue—the white immigrant.[41]

Coolidge's opinion did not reflect dominant views about San Francisco's Italians. Even the immigrant-baiting *American Patriot*, the local organ of the anti-immigrant, anti-Catholic American Protective Association, stressed that "as opposed to the Irish, the heathenish, superstitious ways of Italian immigrants can be overcome."[42] Trappings of Italian culture in San Francisco provoked little criticism among nativists, for the "thrift and industry" of Italians reinforced basic republican qualities and contributed "powerfully to the building up of California."[43]

Italian newcomers were ideally flexible and relevant symbols for contemporary life in San Francisco. As whites in a society which had identified the threat to its values with color, they were generally considered culturally innocuous. Mostly of peasant background, they reassured those who sought links between the basic tenets of American life and a wholesome rural background. Numerically and culturally, Italians appeared as "pre-potent as the Jews," the other dominant group of newcomers to San Francisco.[44] Yet Jews aroused more ambivalent sentiments. Folk fears of the Jew as extortioner, exploiter of working people rather than tiller of the land, did not allow for their smooth matchup with San Francisco's immigrant mystique.

While southern European peasants were esteemed for the important moral benefits they purportedly reaped from their attachment to the soil of Europe, Jews were often associated with destructive heirlooms of the Old World, particularly unscrupulous trading. In rural California, Jewish shopkeepers had a reputation of enticing farmers into the "irretrievable indebtedness" of bond slaves.[45] In San Francisco, a local author compared Jewish merchants to Chinese opium dealers; both traded in the souls of society.[46] At best Jewish merchants served as "trusty thermometers registering financial and commercial conditions," although they refused to sacrifice their own narrow interests "to check disastrous fluctuations in moneyed values or the laying of waste of a country."[47]

All too often the Jew in California was associated with the demented Hebrew presented in the writings of Frank Norris. This fictional character—Knobel was his name in Norris's early works—was the epitome of unwonted rapacity. A penny pinching merchant, Knobel earned his living by preying on the gullibility of his gentile clientele. He lived on Telegraph Hill,

> on a ledge of a big cliff there, and used to lie awake o' windy nights waiting for his house to be blown off that ledge. Knobel had always lived on Telegraph Hill. When he was forty he had had a stroke of paralysis, and had lost the use of his left leg. The result of the stroke was that Knobel was held prisoner on the hill.[48]

Although ostensibly white, Knobel's twisted physique placed him outside the pale of positive immigrants. Ugliness represented moral turpitude, and his physical disability symbolized destructive greed. Knobel's self-entrapment by lust for gold was not a personal problem. His infatuation with money, which held his

52 Signs of Changes

soul hostage on the edge of the cliff, eventually destroyed both him and his predominately gentile victims who had been corrupted by the greed of the merchant. The advent of impoverished newcomers from Russia and Rumania at the turn of the century heightened this image of the Jew. Even sympathetic observers were struck by the demeanor of newly arrived Jewish peddlers who seemed to lack the cultural faculties required by "an advanced state of civilization."[49]

Paradoxically, as the influx of impoverished Jews grew, their public image took a turn for the better. In multifarious San Francisco, where politicians of all stripes sought the immigrant vote and the ancient culture of the Hebrews evoked basically positive images, a more attractive concept of Jews eventually emerged. Improving the stature of Jews required a distancing of Hebrew culture from its singular association with commerce and the adaptation of newcomers to the mold of the Positive Immigrant. Within this context, a local Rabbi, Jacob Voorsanger, suggested that Jews should be considered a "trinity," his metaphor for an individual whose character was sufficiently ambiguous to appeal to everyone. Jews were first Americans, he stated, then natives of venerable European civilizations, and finally members of "the ancient and honorable confraternity of Judaism."[50] Orientation towards getting ahead in life—the American element of the trinity—was balanced by tradition and the tempering force of a Judeo-Christian heritage.

Another solution for forging positive attitudes towards Jews emerged in the ruralization of their image. The Jew as sturdy peasant eventually emerged by tracing the roots of San Francisco's Hebrews to Palestine, where their forefathers had once tilled the soil of a land quite similar in its ecology to that of California.[51] "Inasmuch as Jews have shown remarkable adaptability to business conditions," remarked an observer, "there seems a tremendous field in California for an experiment under ideal conditions to establish Jewish farmers, and have them again dwell under their own vine and fig tree."[52]

Transforming the perennial merchant into peasant stock also represented the first concerted effort by the state to translate popular feelings regarding California's European immigrant population into public policy. In the final days of 1913, the newly established California Commission for Immigration and Housing initiated its operations in the public sphere. In its very first operation, the commission coordinated the establishment of an agricultural settlement for a group of ten Russian Jewish junk dealers.[53] This venture reflected conventional wisdom that sought in the immigrant the personification of a cultural bridge between pristine America and the modern industrial state. The undue attention paid to a relatively small group of newcomers was also part of the trend to appease powerful political groups.

The California State Commission for Immigration and Housing, a public body charged with facilitating the integration of the newcomer into California, was a by-product of the Progressive Party's search for political longevity. Having failed in its bid for the presidency in 1912, the Progressive Party turned its attention to the individual states, hoping to assert its viability by accomplishing party goals at the state level. A rational immigration policy had always been high on the Progressive's list of priorities. Successful implementation of immigrant policies allowed the Progressive party to present itself as an effective alternative to the two major parties.

California, a stronghold of Progressive political power, became the major arena for this effort. While other states, such as New York and Massachusetts, appointed similar bodies to deal with immigrants, the California Commission functioned within a favored political climate and was most effective in obtaining legislative action.[54] A formidable governor and a willing legislature joined hands in devising new social legislation for an industrial society by means of the Immigration Commission. The Commission also excelled in its ability to fuse a wide range of opinions regarding immigrants, from those of suspicious trade unionists to the anti-restrictionist policies of immigration boosters. A willingness to address the needs of diverse groups was due in part to a successful choice of commissioners. It also reflected the efforts of California's Progressives to stymie the erosion of their broad political base.

The year following the presidential elections of 1912 did not augur favorably for California Progressives. By the summer of 1913, a cloud of economic depression and industrial strife darkened the Pacific coast, threatening the party's fragile grasp on the Golden State. A major confrontation between dissatisfied workers and business interests erupted on the large ranches that dominated California's agricultural areas. On the Durst hop ranch, in the heart of Northern California's fertile hinterland, dissatisfied workers led by unionists from the I.W.W.—the radical anti-property Industrial Workers of the World—clashed with sheriff's deputies. California's ranchers, unwilling to address the problems of deceptive labor practices and unsanitary working conditions which had sparked the incident, responded by organizing a militant Farmers' Protective League.[55]

54   Signs of Changes

In the cities, unemployment led to similar polarities, with over seventy thousand idle workingmen stalking the streets of Oakland and San Francisco in the Fall of 1913. Economic distress spurred the formation of a fifteen-hundred-man march on the state's capital in Sacramento. In the eyes of wary business interests, the procession represented a reincarnation of "Coxey's Army," the famous march of the unemployed on Washington in the winter of 1893-1894. Unrest among urban unemployed and fears of an I.W.W. conspiracy spreading from the agricultural areas of the state led to the rise of employers' organizations in Oakland, San Francisco, and other major cities.[56]

Industrial strife threatened to tear the Progressive party apart. Bickering produced schisms and an unexpected defeat of Progressives in the municipal elections of 1913 in Los Angeles, hitherto a bastion of party strength.[57] In San Francisco, the party's powerful pro-labor wing engaged in an acrimonious debate with business oriented Progressives. Hiram Johnson, the state's Progressive governor, was faced with an immediate need to reassert the position of his party as middle ground between labor and capital.

It is within this context that the governor appointed a fact finding commission for dealing with the state's immigration issues which, in the national political arena, had been identified as a major point of contention between labor and capital. With estimates of immigration through the Panama Canal running between 40,000 to 75,000 per year, and an expected influx of 4,000 per month to San Francisco, the Progressives sought to appease fears of job security among the working class without alienating the city's powerful immigrant communities.[58] Political expediency also demanded an acknowledgment of business interests, who hoped to bolster the state's industrial output with a new and somewhat docile immigrant workforce.[59]

On the local level in San Francisco, pragmatic politics demanded a widely acceptable immigration policy. An intelligent and rational policy, it was hoped, would win over both working class voters and immigrants, two very reluctant groups of Progressive supporters. The presidential elections of 1912, had produced miserable results for Progressives in San Francisco, a city dominated by labor and immigrant interests. The Democratic candidate, Woodrow Wilson, had carried the city by ten thousand votes. In the districts south of Market street, heavily populated by blue collar workers and newcomers, the Progressives failed to win a single precinct.[60]

The Progressive party's search for political survival, by providing palatable solutions for burning social issues, induced Governor Hiram Johnson to accept the recommendations of his fact finding committee to establish a permanent body for immigration matters. As a state institution striving for a policy of consensus, the California Commission for Immigration and Housing avoided any clear stand on the delicate issue of federal immigration restrictions. Instead, its commissioners concentrated on resident aliens, particularly those of European origin, who did not arouse passions associated with the state's Asian population. According to the Commission, European newcomers did not present society with any new problems but merely intensified aspects of existing obstacles. As such, solutions to California's problems were not sought in laws or policies that treated immigrants differently than the native born, but by measures which aimed at removing obstacles that set newcomers apart.[61]

A compassion for the immigrant and a willingness to accommodate diverse interest groups were reflected in the Commission's top officials. Ethnically and professionally they represented a broad cross section of California society, living proof that it was feasible to blend subcultures and political interests. The representative of ethnic diversity in the Commission was a Catholic prelate, the Reverend Edward Joseph Hanna, soon to be Archbishop of San Francisco. Well aware of the cultural plurality within his church and in his city, Hanna sought to preserve "the good and the moral," the invaluable fundamental elements that immigrants brought with them to the New World.[62] Hanna directed the Commission's complaints department and information bureaus whose purpose it was to shield the innocent immigrant from exploitation.

Another commissioner monitoring the relationship between society and the alien was Paul Scharrenberg, secretary of California's State Federation of Labor, the umbrella organization for unions affiliated with the American Federation of Labor. Scharrenberg, a German Protestant immigrant and long-time resident of San Francisco, viewed his mission as two fold: guarding against "forgetting the toilers" by a bevy of "university men," and denying businessmen the opportunity of using the Commission as a coordinating agent for importing cheap and docile immigrant labor.[63]

Scharrenberg brought to the Commission an understanding that, despite their zealous guarding of the work place, organized labor harbored no lingering animosity towards European newcomers. When 227 San Francisco labor locals voiced their opinions on the most important legislative needs for workingmen,

56 Signs of Changes

only eight advocated immigration restriction; among these, seven dealt exclusively with Asians.[64] Newcomers and native workers had more in common than was realized, Scharrenberg advocated. Land monopoly and land speculation, the major cause of an unstable job market, appeared high on the list of common concerns shared by immigrant and native workingmen. According to the voice of Labor in the Commission, unfair corporate land assets, not an overabundance of newcomers, caused economic and social instability in California.[65] Only by removing unnatural land monopolies from the market place could the workingman and the newcomer stride together towards establishing permanent and stable domiciles in California.[66]

Sharing labor's concern for social stability among working people were the two southern Californian Commissioners, Mrs. Mary S. Gibson of Los Angeles and Dr. James McBride of Pasadena. Both focused on the creation of a positive domestic environment in which immigrants would emulate American domestic lifestyles. While McBride concentrated on architectural arrangements of the ideal home and aspects of personal hygiene, Gibson emphasized the uplifting of the immigrant mother as linchpin of the family.[67]

The presiding member of the Commission was Simon Lubin, a Jewish merchant and intellectual from Sacramento, heir apparent to the Lubin and Weinstock Dry Goods enterprise, the largest mail order house on the Pacific coast. As personal friend of Governor Johnson, Lubin had been instrumental in creating the Commission and defining its goals. Most of the Commission's legislative initiatives were his own personal creation. Together with his commissioners, he retained his post until October 15, 1923. A Harvard graduate and former settlement worker in Boston's South End Settlement House, Lubin derived his concept of the immigration problem from two influential eastern reformers, Frances Kellor, the head of New York's Bureau of Industrialization and Immigration, and the educator John Foster Carr.[68]

From Kellor, who together with Jane Addams had written the Progressive Party's immigration platform, he adopted the concept of a "domestic immigration policy," a centrally controlled, government-directed program for resident aliens.[69] "Our Commission is not primarily interested in questions of liberal immigration or immigration restriction," he noted, echoing the thoughts of Frances Kellor. "Our chief task is to recommend to the legislature measures that will look toward the care protection and education of the immigrants who have come to us."[70] Based on Kellor's advice, the California Commission avoided a pretentious remaking of the immigrant. Instead, its officers meticulously garnered jurisdiction over a wide range of mundane issues, from a strict enforcement of the sanitary code to the creation of a positive family environment, issues that hitherto had been "ignored" and "belittled" in the zeal to Americanize aliens.[71]

Another of Lubin's mentors, the educator John Foster Carr, strengthened his convictions that there was no viable reason for transforming the fundamental values of the newcomer from Europe. The immigrant often arrived in the New World armed with the basic ideals of "our Republic."[72] He was, in Carr's eyes, already Americanized, particularly in "the national passion" of Europeans to own land.[73] Carr's ideas fell on fertile ground. Lubin had always expressed an admiration for the virtues of the small European landowner and farmer. His father, David Lubin, a Polish born, rags-to-riches Jew, had dedicated his career to championing the cause of the tiller of the land.

As founder of an international organization for agricultural cooperation, the elder Lubin had invested a lifetime in formulating strategies for the survival of the independent peasant farmer. Most of his efforts centered in the Mediterranean basin, which he considered the fountainhead of the American way of life. David Lubin instilled in his son an awareness of the physical similarities between California and the Mediterranean basin, where, in his view, small landowners in Palestine, Greece, and Italy had developed the fundamental concepts of western democracy. California, therefore, seemed an ideal place to launch a concerted, centrally directed project to salvage the values of the Mediterranean-based "aristocrats of the human family."[74]

Firm governmental direction of immigration policy, and a focus on newcomers from the Mediterranean, permeated the policies of the Commission. Having publically committed themselves to the concept that immigrants created no new problems for society, Lubin and his commissioners advanced the cause of the immigrant as prospective farmer. Politically, the alien as agriculturist satisfied diverse interest groups. By distancing newcomers from urban industrial centers, the Commission hoped to placate embattled labor unions, while rural settlement of immigrants partially accommodated the demands of developers and business interests.[75]

However, corporate land monopolies, vicious labor strife in the agricultural sector, and a realistic approach to immigrants' gravitation towards urban centers, eventually encouraged a development of different foci. After establishing headquarters in San Francisco, the state's most luring target for European

58 Signs of Changes

newcomers, the Commission turned its attention to the development of urban housing policies and education programs for California's predominately urban European immigrants.[76] As evident in the commission's choice of its official title, "Housing," rather than settlement—a code word for the unrealistic funneling of immigrants to rural areas—appeared as the most urgent issue confronting Lubin and his colleagues.

The Commission's housing policy expounded a firm belief that "the character of our homes, including those of the humblest and smallest wage earners will determine by and large the character of the state."[77] The promotion of single family dwellings provided a formula for protecting immigrants and their cultural assets. Only within the relative security of a single family abode could newcomers practice the virtues of familial piety, their most vital contribution to America in an industrial age.[78] In their *A.B.C. of Housing*, a compilation of housing guidelines for immigrants and working people, Lubin and his associates urged the maintaining of the classic single family abode for a large spectrum of society through cost-efficient technology.[79]

To perpetuate "the perfectly wholesome instinct and emotions" stemming from the immigrant's heritage, while neutralizing "the many competitors" associated with city life, the home had to cultivate the familiar appearance of the European rural domicile.[80] Indeed, the graphic appearance of homes was no less important than technological improvements and the promise of better living conditions. Plans called for rustic working class cottages and bungalows, whose styles and modes of construction included both the simplicity of rustic cottages and the advances of modern building technology.[81] Like the middle class tract houses in the suburban Bay Area, these homes had certain rural qualities "but were not of it." At the same time they brandished technological improvements associated with city life, "but not of it."[82]

Not model tenements, but detached "one family houses with lawn and room for rear garden" promised to reinforce the positive rural qualities of immigrants.[83] Infusion of distinctly American values would come through the introduction of technology. Streamlined American building techniques assured cheap affordable private space. Modern conveniences, such as plumbing, advanced "social or spiritual assimilation" by attuning immigrants to the lifestyle and fundamental habits practiced in the homes and families of the New World.[84]

Like the very concept of ideal immigrants, a blending of values—rustic and urban, modern and traditional—determined the design of the model homes.

Innumerable variations on the attractive qualities of immigrants could be distilled from this fusion of contradictory elements. Both progress and tradition, stability and commitment to change, permeated the epistemology of the California Commission on Housing and Immigration.

Within the immigrant household, the lifestyle and habits of the mother attracted the Commission's attention. As linchpin of immigrant family life, her unchanging ways and isolation from mainstream society contradicted the flexible guidelines of the Commission's goals.[85] Children became acquainted with American ways through the schools, and the breadwinners through the workplace. The alien mother, restricted to the domestic domain, remained embalmed in her old world habits. This factor posed a threat as "the clever boy or girl who is the hope of the teacher" would display "superiority or contempt" for a "mother who wears a shawl."[86]

In accordance with the general logic governing attitudes towards immigrants, suggestions for uplifting the immigrant mother focused on physical rather than intellectual aspects. Children's contemptuous attitudes, according to Commissioner Gibson, resulted from the outmoded appearance of the immigrant parent. Outlandish lifestyles presented homemakers in a disparaging light. Therefore, Gibson urged an aggressive campaign to bolster the visual image of the "home conserver" by modifying her dress habits, cooking style, and hygiene practices.[87] This, indeed, was the essence of the Commission's "Education at Home" project.[88] To uphold parental discipline, mothers needed to be "in step with the children," a goal which would be accomplished through on-the-spot instruction in the art of maintaining American standards of living.[89]

Visible qualities, both in her home and in her personal appearance, needed modification in order to strengthen the image of the mother. Consequently, the Commission's home teachers encouraged an imitation of American home furnishing and housekeeping methods, thereby exposing immigrant mothers to "the best America has to offer." English lessons for immigrant mothers stressed these values in their texts. A series of "primer lessons" offered by the Commission dwelt on the virtues of wearing nightgowns in bed, the preparation of American meals, and tea party etiquette.[90]

The attention given to immigrant mothers, besides addressing the needs of this particular group, furnished a fitting metaphor for contemporary cultural trends. San Franciscans at the turn of the century were not looking for the larger than life, but the normal; not the herald of a new age, but the embodiment of

60   Signs of Changes

contemporary times; not the flamboyant genius, but the ordinary person possessing commonplace virtues to an extraordinary degree. Attitudes towards immigrants from Europe constituted a projection of the positive aspects of the California self. Ordinary Californians expected newcomers to be pretty much like themselves. The concept of the ideal immigrant, flexible enough to appeal to both ordinary worker or middle class businessman, was an idealized version of San Franciscans' own multifarious autobiographies.

On a practical level, the policies of the Commission for Immigration and Housing diminished uncertainty over immigrant policy among various sectors of society. For established blue collar workers, common policy for both immigrants and native laborers ensured future strength and attenuated fears of clashes with immigrants in an inundated job market. Furthermore, accessible, state-directed housing projects, which represented the most tangible fruits of American democracy, augured well for a growing sense of common goals, too.

For immigrants, the Commission offered a sense of identity through an acceptance of some of their fundamental qualities. As demands for change were mostly superficial and concentrated on their appearance and public conduct, immigrants could realize their growing expectations by adjusting their public mannerisms to the code of modern city dwellers. As for the established middle class which had created the Commission, a state apparatus allowed them to imbue immigrants with certain cosmetic changes, thereby removing fears of foreign cultural blemishes from their concept of American society.

Simon Lubin, the Commission's founder and catalyst, had a personal stake in the fruition of all these goals. As a successful businessman, the rise of ethnic, economic, and social tensions challenged his status in society. As the son of an immigrant, maintaining the dignity of the newcomer while demanding only cosmetic changes fulfilled a personal need. As a Jew, he had an immediate interest in transforming the image of his co-religionists into an acceptable form.

A prominent member of the state's established Jewry, Simon Lubin shared the concerns of community leaders for eliminating the visible peculiarities of Jews and bringing them into line with their fellow citizens. Lubin and many other Jewish supporters of the Progressive party advocated state directed solutions. But in San Francisco, where most Jewish newcomers gathered, individual Hebrew congregations aligned themselves with contemporary culture on their own volition. Always sensitive to vacillating cultural trends, the established Jewish communities of San Francisco placed great emphasis on the adjustment of visual mannerisms. The status of all Jews, they felt, hinged upon newcomers' acceptance of these demands.

The behavioral changes advocated by the dominant society appealed to Jews as they did to other ethnic groups within San Francisco. Culture, as a tool for forging meaning out of mundane experience, was enhanced through the existence of superficial, therefore, malleable boundaries. Indeed, the acceptance of commonly held codes of conduct gave rootless immigrants and transplanted Americans a common sense of belonging without demanding ethnic capitulation.

62   Signs of Changes

Notes

1. Robert Louis Stevenson and Lloyd Osborne, *The Wrecker* (New York, New Edition, 1923), 158.
2. James Bryce, *The American Commonwealth* (New York, New Edition, 1911), 428.
3. United States Census Bureau, *Eleventh Census; Abstract* (Second Revised and Enlarged Edition, Washington D.C., 1896), Vol.10, table 43; *Compendium of the Eleventh Census 1890* (Washington, D.C., 1894), Vol.1, 541-580; *ibid.*, Vol.2, 604. On immigration and the Panama Canal see U.S. House of Representatives, *Restriction of Immigration; Hearing before the Committee on Immigration and Naturalization on H. R. 6060. Statement of Frank Morris, Secretary of American Federation of Labor* (Washington, D.C., 1914).
4. For a discussion of migratory trends in California see Moses Rischin, "Immigration, Migration, and Minorities in California: a Reassessment," *Pacific Historical Review*, 41 (Feb., 1972), 71-90.
5. Robert Watchorn, "Draft of Report by California Immigration Committee to Governor Johnson," (Feb. 14, 1913), Simon Lubin papers, Bancroft Library, box 3.
6. A highly interpretive overview of anti-Chinese sentiment may be found in Alexander Saxton, *The Indispensable Enemy; Labor and the Anti-Chinese Movement in California* (Berkeley, 1971). Gunther Barth, *Bitter Strength; A History of the Chinese in the United States; 1850-1870* (New York, 1961), provides indispensable background for an understanding of anti-Chinese sentiment in San Francisco in the late nineteenth century.
7. On anti-Japanese agitation see Roger D. Daniels, *The Politics of Prejudice; The Anti-Japanese Movement in California and the Struggle for Japanese Exclusion* (Berkeley, 1962).
8. On the San Francisco ordinance discriminating against aliens see *L'Italia*, August 25, 1911.
9. The San Francisco context of fashioning cultural heroes in the image of their creators is discussed in John W. Caughey, *Hubert Howe Bancroft; Historian of the West* (New York, 1946), 314-316. For an overview of the distinctly white complexion of American pioneering and expansionism see Frederick Merk, *Manifest Destiny and Mission in American History* (New York, 1963),

Albert Weinberg, *Manifest Destiny; a Study of National Expansionism in American History* (Gloucester, Mass., 1958).

10. John Seelye, "Horatio Alger Out West; A Marriage of Myths, "introduction to Horatio Alger, *The Young Miner* (San Francisco, New Edition, 1965), xi.

11. San Francisco *Call*, May 8, 1900, 12.

12. On Japanese efforts to emulate White Americans see Bureau of Labor Statistics, *Ninth Biennial Report, 1899-1900* (Sacramento, 1900), 34-35.

13. "The World's Most Menacing Problem," *California Outlook*, 14 (May 31, 1913), 6. This article is a reprint from *Collier's*.

14. Bureau of Labor Statistics, *First Biennial Report, 1883-4* (Sacramento, 1884), 10; California State Federation of Labor, *Proceedings of the Fourteenth Annual Convention in Fresno* (Fresno, 1914), 74-76.

15. Douglas H. Daniels, *Pioneer Urbanites; A Social and Cultural History of Blacks in San Francisco* (Philadelphia, 1980), 84. For an excellent discussion of popular portrayals of the urban black, the "Jim Dandy", see Lewis A. Erenberg, *Steppin' Out; New York Nightlife and the Transformation of Urban Culture, 1890-1930* (Westport, Conn., 1981), 19. An example of the San Francisco stage's portrayal of blacks appears in San Francisco *Wave*, 16 (June 26, 1897), 10-11.

16. Bernard Moses, "On Our Government; National Power" (Sept. 28, 1894), Bernard Moses papers, Bancroft Library carton 2. See also Hubert H. Bancroft, "Two Sides of a Vexed Question," *Essays and Miscellany*, 38 (San Francisco, 1890), 237, 243, 278.

17. Commission of Immigration and Housing, "Immigrant Education, "*Second Annual Report* (Sacramento, 1916), 143.

18. Douglas Daniels, *Pioneer Urbanites*, 42-43; Spencer C. Olin, "European Immigrants and Oriental Aliens; Acceptance and Rejection by the California Legislature of 1913," *Pacific Historical Review*, 35 (August, 1966), 303-315. Anti-Asian sentiments in the market place are discussed in Bureau of Labor Statistics, *Ninth Biennial Report*, 66-71.

19. Hubert H. Bancroft, "Adolph Gustav Russ," *Chronicles of the Builders*, 7 vols. (San Francisco, 1892), V, 533-542.

20. A short summary of the German re-writing of the history of California appears in Erwin G. Gudde, *German Pioneers in Early California* (Hoboken, N. J., 1927).

21. Olin, "European Immigrants and Oriental Aliens," 303-305.

64 Signs of Changes

22. For an example of contemporary assessments of European immigrants as inferiors see Cora Powell, "A Mental Survey of the Three Lowest Grades in One of San Francisco's Most Difficult Elementary Schools" (M.A., Berkeley, 1920). On European immigrants as economic threats see: *Call*, June 19, 1897, 4.

23. The expected concentration of immigrants in large cities, particularly San Francisco is assessed in Simon Lubin to Egisto Rossi (March 25, 1914), Simon Lubin papers, Bancroft Library, box 4. For census reports on immigration trends see, California Commission for Immigration and Housing, *Second Annual Report*, 309; United States Bureau of the Census, *Abstract of the Thirteenth Census* (Washington, D.C., 1913), 95, table 19.

24. Society of the Sons of the American Revolution, *Annual Banquet; Washington's Birthday, February 22, 1898* (San Francisco, 1898), 3, Bernard Moses Papers, Bancroft Library, carton 3.

25. For an example of animosity towards San Franciscans who cherished exclusive backgrounds see "Dedication of James Lick Monument," San Francisco Board of Supervisors, *Municipal Reports, 1893-1894* (San Francisco, 1894), 252-253.

26. Elizabeth G. Potter, Mabel Thayer Gray, *The Lure of San Francisco* (San Francisco, 1915), 14. On the enshrining of Hispanic culture in California see Hubert H. Bancroft, *California Pastoral* (San Francisco, 1888).

27. Potter and Gray, *The Lure of San Francisco*, 85-86; Joseph A. Dunn, *Carefree San Francisco* (San Francisco, 1905), 115.

28. Samuel H. Scudder, "The Californian of the Future," *Overland Monthly*, 19 (April 1892), 385-386.

29. Simon J. Lubin, "The Contribution of the Nations to American Ideals; Address delivered at the First Annual Lincoln's Birthday International Musical and Folk Festival, Held under the Auspices of the Immigration Department of the San Francisco Y.M.C.A." (N. P., 1913), Simon Lubin papers, Bancroft Library, carton 1. A forceful nativist statement on physiogenics appears in U. S. Senate, *Immigration Commission Report, 1910-1911*, 43-44.

30. This typical description of San Francisco as the Mediterranean of the New World is from *Program for the Fifth International Convention of the Epworth League in San Francisco* (San Francisco, 1901). See also Bernard Moses, "California, Opportunity in Matters of Education; Address to Harvard Club

of San Francisco" (October 19, 1893), Bernard Moses papers, Bancroft Library, carton 1; Hubert H. Bancroft, "Ideas Occasioned by a Proposal to Hold a Pacific Coast Historical Exhibition in Sacramento in 1892" (Ms., Bancroft library), 23-24.

31. Simon Lubin to Martin Madsen (February 7, 1914), Simon Lubin papers, Bancroft Library box, 4; William P. Shriver, "Immigrants on the Pacific Coast," *Immigrants in America Review*, 1 (September, 1915), 81-82.

32. Samuel Vitone, "Community Identity and Schools; Educational Experiences of Italians in San Francisco, from the Gold Rush to the Second World War" (Ph.D., Berkeley, 1981), 243-247, 282. Victor L. Shrader, "Ethnic Politics, Religion, and the Public Schools of San Francisco, 1849-1973" (Ph.D., Stanford, 1974),97-101.

33. *Call*, March 3, 1909, 11. On disparaging attitudes towards ethnocentricity see *Call*, August 31, 1902, 22.

34. On anti-Asian sentiment see California Bureau of Labor Statistics, *Ninth Biennial Report*, 108-111. Attitudes towards literacy tests are discussed in *Proceedings of Western Labor Immigrant Conference Held in Labor Temple, Seattle Washington, November 1913* (Tacoma, Wa., 1913), 14-16.

35. On McCarthy's distribution of electoral material in Hebrew see *Jewish Times and Observer*, November 1, 1907, 9.

36. *Call*, Sept 9, 1903, 21. Winfield Scott, "Old Wine in New Bottles," *Sunset Magazine*, 30 (May, 1913), 519-520.

37. For a pro-Labor report on the Italian Bakers Union struggle see *Call*, February 2, 1908, 36. Dino Cinel, *From Italy To San Francisco; The Immigrant Experience* (Stanford, 1982), 115, 282, presents a different interpretation of the attitude of organized labor towards Italian immigrants. Note that Cinel deals with skilled trade unions rather than labor unions in general.

38. California State Federation of Labor, *Seventh Annual Convention Proceedings* (Stockton, 1907), 62-63, 83, 87, 91; *Twelfth Annual Convention Proceedings* (Bakersfield, 1911), 69.

39. The *Wasp* cited in *L'Italia*, November 9, 1903.

40. Scott, "Old Wines in New Bottles, ", 519-520.

41. Mary Roberts Coolidge, *Chinese Immigration* (New York, 1909), 74, 456.

66 Signs of Changes

42. *American Patriot*, October 11, 1894, 6. See also *La Voce Del Popolo*, September 25 1895, in which this San Francisco Italian newspaper praises the *American Patriot* for its positive attitude towards local Italians.

43. Obert F. Simpson, *Wake Up Americans; Address to American Colony in San Francisco* (San Francisco, 19--), 27.

44. Scott, "Old Wine in New Bottles, " 527.

45. Robert Louis Stevenson, "Monterey," in James Hart (ed.), *From Scotland to Silverado. By Robert Louis Stevenson* (New York, 1966), 162.

46. Grant Carpenter, "The Claws of The Dragon; The Official, The Jew, and The Prophet," *Sunset Magazine*, 30 (March 1913), 305-314. See also Grace Helen Bailey, "The Jew," *Overland Monthly*, 45 (March, 1905), 193-195.

47. K. M. Nesfeld, "The Jew From a Gentile Standpoint," *Overland Monthly*, 8 (April 1895), 410-411; Hubert H. Bancroft, *California Inter Pocula*, 35 (San Francisco, 1889), 372-374.

48. Frank Norris, "Judy's Service of Gold Plate," in *Frank Norris of The Wave* (San Francisco, 1931), 55-56. This short story was the basis for the character Zerkow in Norris's *Mc Teague*.

49. Nesfeld, "The Jew From a Gentile Viewpoint", 410.

50. Jacob Voorsanger, "The Trinity of Political Independence," in Sons of the American Revolution, *Annual Banquet, 1898*, 19. See also Jacob Voorsanger, "Immigration," *Emanu-El*, February 24, 1911, 4.

51. On the Jew as farmer see E. F. Gerecht, "The Jewish Immigrant as Tiller of the Soil," *California Outlook*, 16 (January 3, 1914), 8-9; Charles Fleisher, "The Jew," *California Outlook*, 1 4 (May 24, 1913), 14-15. On the similarities between Palestine and California see: Bernard Moses, "California, Opportunities in Matters of Education."

52. Robert W. Lynch, "Agricultural Opportunities For Jewish Immigrants in California," *Emanu-El*, April 5, 1912, 14.

53. Mary Gibson to Dr. Parker, December 18, 1913, Dr. Parker to Mary Gibson, December 20, 1913, Simon Lubin papers, Bancroft Library, Box 2.

54. For a positive assessment of legislation for immigrants in California see Public School Education, *Immigrant in America Review*, 1 (June 1915), 7-8.

55. George E. Mowry, *The California Progressives* (Berkeley, 1951), 199-204.

56. *Ibid*; "The Army of The Unemployed in The State Capital", *California Outlook*, 16 (March 21, 1914), 10-11; California State Commission on

Ron Robin 67

Immigration and Housing, *Report On The Relief of Destitute Unemployed, 1914-1915* (Sacramento, 1915), 16.

57. "Results of The Los Angeles Elections," *California Outlook*, 14 (June 7, 1913), 5.

58. On immigration estimates to California see Dr. Francis Parker to Simon Lubin, March 24, 1914, Simon Lubin to Martin Madsen, February 7, 1914, Simon Lubin papers, box 4.

59. Examples of businessmens' desires for increased immigration are expressed in Robert Lynch, "Manufacturers and Immigration on The Pacific Coast," Lenz, *Immigration*, 20-23; "Statement by Commissioner John P. Mc. Laughlin," Bureau of Labor Statistics, *Fifth Biennial Report* (Sacramento, 1892), 48.

60. Alexander P. Saxton, "San Francisco Labor and The Populist and Progressive Insurgencies," *Pacific Historical Quarterly*, 34 (November, 1965), 421-438.

61. Robert Watchorn to Simon Lubin, "Draft by California Commission of Immigration to Governor Johnson (February 14, 1913), Simon Lubin papers, Bancroft Library, box 3.

62. Edward Joseph Hanna to Simon Lubin, December 8, 1914, Simon Lubin papers, Bancroft Library, box 1.

63. Dr. Parker to Simon Lubin, December 18, 1913, Simon Lubin papers, Bancroft Library, box 1; Paul Scharrenberg, "Reminiscences" (Ms., Bancroft Library), 67-69.

64. Bureau of Labor Statistics, *Ninth Biennial Report, 1899-1900*, 108-111.

65. Paul Scharrenberg to George Bell, September 3, 1915, Simon Lubin papers, Bancroft Library, box 3.

66. James W. Mullen, "Land and Labor and Immigration," in Lenz, *Immigration*, 16-17. Mullen was editor of the San Francisco *Labor Clarion*. On the importance of home ownership among the working class see Bureau of Labor Statistics, *Third Biennial Report* (Sacramento, 1888), 67-79.

67. On the Commission's officers and the division of labor among them see Samuel E. Wood, The California State Commission of Immigration and Housing; a Study of Administrative Organization (Ph.D., Berkeley, 1942), 113-119.

68. *Ibid.*, 82-89.

68 Signs of Changes

69. Frances Kellor, "Immigrants in America, a Domestic Policy, *Immigrants in America Review*, 1 (March 1915), 9-10. The impact of Kellor on the California Commission is delineated in Simon Lubin to Frances Kellor, October 18, 1913, Simon Lubin papers, Bancroft Library, box 4.
70. Simon Lubin to Cyrus L. Sultzberger, August 23, 1912, Simon Lubin papers, Bancroft Library, box 4.
71. Ira Cross, "The Immigration Problem," Lenz, *Immigration*, 7.
72. "Immigration Education Society -- Prospectus," John Carr, editor (Circa 1913), Simon Lubin papers, Bancroft Library, box 2.
73. John Foster Carr to Robert Lynch (circa 1914), Simon Lubin papers, Bancroft Library, box 2.
74. Olivia Rossetti Agresti, *David Lubin; A Study in Practical Idealism* (Revised Edition, Berkeley, 1941), 81-145.
75. Labor's views regarding the rural settlement of immigrants are aired in Mullen, "Land, and Labor, and Immigrants." The interests of business are expressed in Robert N. Lynch, "Immigration," *Sunset*, 31 (March, 1914), 593-601. On the commission's efforts to avoid treating immigrants as the creators of special problems see: Commission of Immigration and Housing, *First Annual Report, January 2, 1915* (Sacramento, 1915), 10; ----. *Report on Relief of Destitute Unemployed 1914-1915* (Sacramento, 1915).
76. The prospects of immigrants in California cities in general and San Francisco in particular are discussed in a letter from Simon Lubin to Egisto Rossi, March 25, 1914, Simon Lubin papers, Bancroft Library, box 4.
77. Watchorn, "Draft of Report."
78. Katharine Felton to Simon Lubin, November 1912, Simon Lubin papers, Bancroft Library, box 2.
79. California Commission of Immigration and Housing, *An A.B.C. of Housing* (Sacramento, 1915).
80. Simon Lubin to Robert Lynch, October 23, 1912, Simon Lubin papers, Bancroft Library, box 4; Simon J. Lubin, "Housing and the Immigration Commission," *California Outlook*, 17 (September 5, 1914), 12.
81. California Commission of Immigration and Housing, *First Annual Report*, 97.
82. E.J. Wickson, "Suburban Life in California," *California's Magazine, Edition de Luxe* (San Francisco, 1916), 32-38.
83. *A.B.C. of Housing*, 5-6.

Ron Robin   69

84. *Ibid.*; Simon J. Lubin, "Housing and the Immigration Commission," *California Outlook*, 17 (September 5, 1914), 12; Katharine Felton to Simon Lubin, November 1912, Simon Lubin papers, Bancroft Library, box 2.
85. Kate Waller Barrett, "The Immigrant Woman," in Lenz, *Immigration*, 9-13.
86. Mrs. Krank A. Gibson, "Educating Parents -- A California Problem," *California Outlook*, 18 (February 6, 1915), 9-10; Mary S. Gibson, "The Immigrant Woman," *California Outlook*, 16 (May 9, 1914), 6-7. Note that Mary Gibson and Mrs. Frank Gibson are different pen names for the same person.
87. *Ibid.*.
88. California Commission for Immigration and Housing. *The Home Teacher; The Act, With a Working Plan for Forty Lessons* (Sacramento, 1916).
89. Gibson, "Educating Parents"; Richard K. Campbell, "Home Instruction and Naturalization," California Commission of Immigration and Housing, *Second Annual Report*, 147-148.
    "Working Plans for the Home Teacher," California Commission of Immigration and Housing, *Second Annual Report*, 156, 158.
90. "Suggestions for Teacher," *ibid.*, 13-59.

CHAPTER 3
SAN FRANCISCO'S JEWS AND THE ARCHITECTURE
OF SYMBOLIC ETHNICITY

Travelers approaching San Francisco in the late 1860s would often pause to admire the curious selection of structures towering above the city's horizon. Gaunt windmills, rising thirty feet high and crowned with hovering fan-wheels, were interspersed among gaudy commercial palaces in a fascinating mixture of cultural metaphors. Peering eerily over fog banks, stilted church spires of many denominations stretched alongside conical sand hills of strange and ever-shifting shapes as testimony to the city's apparently endless number of "peculiarities, nationalities, and novelties."[1]

Perceptive observers would most certainly discern a pair of circular "shot towers" towering above the skyline. Like flags of a distant nation, their bulbous domes announced a proud foreign presence within the midst of a bustling American city. A closer look at the edifice beneath the massive towers would reveal a facade blanketed with Stars of David in proclamation of the Hebraic roots of this foreign mission. The "gothic-byzantine" building hidden behind the ostentatious entrance allowed the uninitiated to deduce that the structure—foreign in its towers, Jewish by decoration—was a house of worship.[2] Temple Emanu-El on Sutter Street, with its outlandish flagpole towers, Hebraic adornments, and pedantic ecclesiastical architecture, was the prayer-house of San Francisco's Jewish elite. (Figure 8)

Dedicated in 1866, the imposing edifice underwent radical stylistic mutation as San Francisco moved from its individualistic gold-rush mentality towards conformity with the mores of urban-industrial America. With the passage of time, and aided by natural calamities, flagpole towers were lowered, Hebraic adornments were softened, and the temple's design shifted away from overtly Jewish connotations. Congregation Emanu-El was not alone in its adjustment to urban ways. Other established Jewish congregations in the city followed suit. Design and ornament in affluent city temples were not rigid cultural statements, but formulas for smooth transition in a process of rapid urbanization.

As the morphology of local synagogues adjusted itself to the changing times, so, too, the Jewish press also re-wrote the history of Jewish presence in California. Early editions of the Jewish press had emphasized the unique cultural background and economic skills of Jews in California. By the turn of the century, and in accordance with popular disaffection with maverick behavior, Jews reappeared as humble California pioneers, no better, no worse, than their gentile neighbors.

Even impoverished Jewish newcomers of a mostly eastern European origin who had begun to trickle into the Bay Area in the closing years of the nineteenth century, recognized the need for continuous change. Established Jews expressed their creed clearly and visibly in community newspapers and through symbolic redesigning of their ornate temples. Indigent newcomers, in make-shift synagogues and deprived of elaborate literary skills, utilized less obvious and more personal expressions of their relationship to their milieu, particularly through changes in their religious rituals. By the early twentieth century, the accommodating traditions of newcomers and veterans had produced a common concept of Judaism that strengthened ties with their temporal surroundings by selectively loosening moorings to age-old traditions. Modification of ethnic allegiances among Jews, above and beyond their peculiarly Jewish ramifications, provided a clear commentary on the vertiginous nature of American urban culture. Retention of portable elements of Jewish culture illustrated how an urban population on the move turned relics of a distant past to new purposes in order to synthesize attitudes to match the world view of a new social order.

The harbingers of these pliant notions of Judaism in San Francisco were predominately German-speaking Jewish peddlers and artisans from the villages of Bavaria and Posen, the present-day Polish province of Poznan.[3] Chafing under the burden of discriminatory taxes and humiliating personal restrictions, they descended on the shores of the United States beginning in the late 1830s. Most newcomers took up familiar trades along the eastern seaboard and in the Ohio valley, although a few smaller groups were attracted to the far west.[4] The urban expansion of this particular period in the United States provided accessible economic opportunity for Jewish immigrant-peddlers who already possessed rudimentary urban skills. In turn, economic incentive encouraged the growth of the seeds of religious revisionism to which they had been exposed in Europe. Religious reform complemented entrepreneurship, for both accepted change as a necessary element for survival.

Even without delving into the complexities of the reform movement, the radical differences between Reform practices and orthodoxy are quite obvious.[5] Traditional Judaism, as practiced in Europe, derived its authority from written accounts of rabbinical debates about Mosaic law which took place between the second and sixth centuries B.C. Known as the Talmud, this accumulation of Biblical interpretation not only defined fundamental religious practices; every conceivable mode of behavior, from modes of dress to detailed dietary practices, received rigid, intractable canonization. Talmudic principles asserted that the customs of a sacred people demanded strict adherence so as to set Jews apart from the nations of the world. This internal predisposition for isolation was sustained by existing political and social constellations in Europe. Until the Napoleonic wars spread notions of individual emancipation and equality, Jews formed separate entities in a predominantly Christian and feudalistic Europe. Their community structures usually received official sanction as legal internal governing bodies. Within the boundaries prescribed by rulers and princes, Jews were left to their own communal devices.

The rise of nationalism sparked off by the French Revolution and the Napoleonic wars disrupted these timeless precepts. Nationalism encouraged Jews, particularly in urban areas, to perceive of themselves as emancipated citizens of a loosely defined Jewish persuasion, not unlike their gentile counterparts who were affiliated with a variety of Christian sects. Emancipation challenged the essence of orthodoxy which held Jews to be a separate people, a nation within nations. In breaching the walls of tradition, orthodox rituals, in particular, came under attack. Elevating Judaism to the status of a gentrified religion required the abandoning of medieval customs of worship and daily behavior. Eloquent reformers, preaching from the urbane pulpits of large German cities, demanded change in visual and public aspects of Judaism. The spontaneous chanting in a foreign tongue gave way to Protestant-like, centrally-directed hymn singing; family worship replaced traditionally segregated and predominantly male congregations. Modified liturgy inevitably affected the realm of thought, too. Jewish intellectuals attracted to reform assumed that a progressive religion should preach humanistic values and that interpreters of the Talmud had mistakenly sanctified ritual rather than content. In their eyes, the moral preachings of the prophets, not the legal portions of the scriptures, constituted the heart of Judaism.

Jewish peddlers and artisans from the villages of central Europe, who made up the bulk of newcomers to America, were by no means swept away by the intricacies of reform. Yet having compared their oppressive circumstances to the promises of emancipation, they embraced any attempt, secular or religious, to ameliorate social isolation and economic repression. When, in the wake of

Napoleonic defeats in the 1830s and 1840s, economic stagnation and the restoration of religious discrimination resurrected medieval limitations on their freedom, growing numbers of Jews opted for the relatively open horizons of America. With them, they carried the seeds of religious reform.

In America, where Judaism had no legal standing, religious revisionism achieved even greater success than it had in the German states. Neither tight communal boundaries nor entrenched rabbinical establishments challenged innovation. In the United States, each synagogue was an island unto itself thereby weakening the hold of orthodoxy. No widely accepted body supervised basic communal rites such as the ritual slaughter of edible animals. No beacon light illuminated the path of Jewish education or the organization and operation of charities. Lacking a central leadership, split into independent houses of worship, and divested of a consolidated communal structure, Jewish orthodoxy failed to retain the hearts and minds of ambitious, commercially-minded aspirants from the stifling milieu of Central Europe.

As rootless persons in the amorphous environment of mid-century America, German Jews fashioned pliant forms of worship which encouraged social adaptation to a fluid American society.[6] Intellectually, they cast aside their destiny as one community bound together by messianic ties to their biblical homeland. Reform offered a more secure form of identity because it lacked immutable connections to a remote culture. Eventually, revised prayer books abandoned the use of Hebrew, deleted all references to the Jewish people's ultimate return to Zion, and, conversely, emphasized the role of Jews as forerunners of universal justice and brotherly love. Judaism, according to the definitive platform of Reform, preached "postulates of reason," ever-capable of modification in accordance with the advance of human knowledge.[7] Outdated Orthodox rituals were abandoned; so was "any national aim or national character of Judaism."[8]

Reform found firm, inviting terrain in San Francisco. The Jewish peddlers who had converged on the Bay Area discovered that revisionism provided solutions above and beyond the sphere of religion. By removing elements of restraint, Reform Judaism complemented economic and social freedom by encouraging desires to shape, not only to adapt to, new surroundings. Like most newcomers, San Francisco's Jews were attracted to California by the lure of gold; unlike their peers, they avoided mining. Most chose peddling and petty trading as they had done in Europe and east of the Rockies. In the long run, their

74 Signs of Changes

decision proved wise. Conservative investments in trade weathered the uncertain storms of recurring recessions and turbulent mining prospects. Between 1851 and 1860 German-born San Franciscans more than doubled their mean assets from 11,500 to 31,500, exceeding the accomplishments of both native and other foreign born merchants. Well over half of these German merchants were Jews.[9] Jews were not only predominant in commerce and trading. They also represented a substantial portion of the general population. In gold rush San Francisco, with its innumerable ethnic groups and subcultures, approximately nine percent of the population were German Jews. Only New York had a higher density of Jews at mid-century.[10]

Within the internal confines of San Francisco's Jewish community, and despite acceptance of change, old world regional schisms persisted. Bavarian Jews, the self-styled elite of the city's Jewry, set themselves apart and formed the Congregation Emanu-El. Others, mostly Poles and Poseners, belonged to a rival congregation, Sherith Israel. While both bodies paid lip service to orthodox traditions during their incipient stages, more liberal interpretations soon infiltrated their texture. Two other congregations of the Jewish establishment, Ohabei Shalom and Beth Israel, were formed by local Jews who accepted change, but repudiated an indiscriminate rejection of orthodoxy. Not one of the city's major temples observed strict orthodox traditions.[11]

During the second half of the nineteenth century and through 1915, communal life of the Jewish establishment evolved primarily around these four houses of worship. Through lavish iconographic displays, the various congregations visually reiterated their interpretations of Judaism in the Far West. Emanu-El, the temple frequented by the merchant elite, displayed the most eloquent signs of cultural creed. Having benefitted immensely from the opportunities of the American city, Emanu-El's congregants displayed acute sensitivity to changing cultural tides. Thus, as San Francisco moved from an infatuation with the values of its maverick founders to a celebration of the virtues associated with standardized urbanization, Emanu-El's symbolism changed accordingly.

Emanu-El's most memorable edifice was its opulent Sutter street temple, dedicated in 1866. Neither postcards of city sights, nor booster brochures were complete without vistas of the ostentatious temple and its Moresque towers. (Figure 8) Built during a period in which San Franciscans still flaunted their heterogeneous origins, the building extolled signs of success and Jewish uniqueness. "In point of wealth and grandeur," noted a contemporary observer, it "might be taken for Solomon's Temple."[12]

The San Francisco of 1866, the year in which the Sutter Street temple was consecrated, was in a state of transition. In the popular mind, if not in reality, the city still had about it the aura of a boom town with its motley people singularly engrossed in cultivating their private economic goals. Yet at the same time, class distinctions had already etched themselves into the city's texture. A well-defined merchant elite was in the process of consolidating both economic and political power and had asserted its privileged position by creating genteel, sequestered neighborhoods. The architecture of temple Emanu-El blended quite well into this transitional stage. On the one hand, it was a celebration of particularistic values reminiscent of the gold rush. At the same time it served as an exclusive sanctuary for a powerful faction within the city's merchant elite.

Both architectural design and religious emblems signaled the cultural significance of Temple Emanu-El. The architecture deserves special attention because it expounded the perceived relationship between the congregation and its surroundings. Conversely, the building's adornments, its emblems of religion, signified a hierarchy of internal Jewish values. The prominence, shape and size of these emblems represented a self-conscious definition of self-image.

The eclectic architecture of the temple was a typical creation of its Californian circumstances. San Francisco, the building suggested, was the proverbial Tabula Rasa which would eventually be made over in the image of its beholders. The temple's status as a fellow interloper in a society of intruders was defined by its peculiar foreign appearance and the equally idiosyncratic cityscape upon which it had been deposited. It infringed upon the landscape, and was quite out of context with the topography of the Bay area. Neither building materials, nor style had more than a fleeting connection with the natural surroundings. Like the majority of San Franciscans, the temple approached its environment as if it was a wilderness with no redeeming qualities beyond its economic bounty.

Two competing perspectives of self-image were embedded in the structure. On the one hand, the exclusive ethnic nature of the congregation was defined by prominent religious symbols. At the same time, the architectural design of the structure celebrated the values of an upstart merchant class which transcended any particular religious denomination. Precedence was given to visual displays of Jewish cultural orientation. Moresque towers caught one's initial attention, announcing far and wide an exotic presence transplanted from a distant and

76 Signs of Changes

fabled soil. The golden bulbs perched upon the star-studded towers celebrated the "unparalleled industry and perseverance" of a distinctly foreign community of peddlers turned affluent merchants. Their sheer height—165 feet—proclaimed proud "fealty to the ancestral faith."[13] A swollen facade concealed most of the building below the towers. Like a modern-day billboard, the facade confronted onlookers with a screen of splattered symbols of ethnic identity. Overlooking the facade, and placed between the two towers, stood a representation of the Tablets of the Law, symbol of timeless adherence to ancient rituals. The corpulent facade and shimmering towers were covered with Stars of David. Numerous evenly-spaced minarets flanked the entire building; they too, were adorned with Hebraic emblems.

At the same time, the temple also testified to the success of a multi-denominational merchant class. The mixture of fundamental romanesque architecture, gothic elements of style, and pseudo-oriental turrets placed the building within a broad multi-cultural perspective. Wealth was not the sole domain of Jews, but of a new society made up of a variety of civilizations to which the eclectic architecture of temple Emanu-El was a monument. The opulent structure, with its golden bulbs and pedantic ornamentation celebrated the skills, wealth and acumen of San Francisco's polyglot merchant elite, of which the members of Congregation Emanu-El were an integral part.

Pliable arrangements within the temple softened even further the foreign impressions of the Jewish symbols of the exterior. In departure from the ethnocentricity of the temple's facade, various fixtures and practices within the building suggested that the congregation fashioned itself according to the cultural climate of the day and that it would not resist modification. "Reform calls loud attention to the transient nature of religion," noted Rabbi Jacob Voorsanger, Temple Emanu-El's prelate and self-appointed spokesman for the city's Jewry between the years 1889 and 1908. "Forms of worship of God must change with the spirit of the generation," he added, alluding to his temple's emphasis on flexible religion.[14]

In the spirit of Liberal Protestantism, and motivated by positive assessments of change, the prelates of Emanu-El increasingly preached a fluid moral order rather than the sanctifying of intransigent parochial practices. Weekly sermons drifted away from theoretical treatises of Jewish law towards broad humanistic issues. By the turn of the century it was not uncommon for reform rabbis to replace religious sermons with sedate lectures on matters such as the "evils of bad

Ron Robin 77

temper and how to cure it."[15] Friday-night sermons, the principal rostrum for rabbis to expound their views, were often filled with guest lectures on such subjects as the moral qualities of the German-Jewish poet, Heinrich Heine.[16] Occasional union services with liberal Christian congregations strengthened convictions that this congregation of affluent Jews was an integral part of the city's merchant elite.[17]

Gravitation towards genteel religion also dominated the by-laws of Emanu-El. In its zeal to eradicate static orthodox customs, the congregation adopted a complicated ritual of its own, governing the minutest points of etiquette within the prayer hall. Florid Friday night prayer services demanded an entire booklet which resembled a playscript in its allocation of roles and lines to be read by participants.[18] High Holiday services were even more elaborate. Hired musicians and prestigious opera singers participated in controlled, choreographed performances which left little room for spontaneous spiritual expressions of orthodox modes of worship.[19] To enhance the aesthetic impact of musical renditions during High Holiday services, female congregants broke with time-honored decorum by removing their hats, "because it would help the acoustics of the synagogues."[20] These musical extravaganzas, which interspersed traditional Jewish melodies with classical masterpieces, conveyed a transcendental, non-sectarian interpretation of Judaism. When exposed to these melodious incantations, even a gentile observer could exclaim "I could worship very well in a synagogue with the help of the ministry of music."[21]

The internal design of the temple reflected the tendency towards revisionism, too. Although Jewish symbols decorated interior doorways and walls, the prayer hall betrayed vestiges of a gentrified, almost Protestant style of worship. Female worshippers and children were still restricted to a gallery overlooking the main worship hall, but little else recalled any sense of orthodoxy. The traditional Bimah, the elevated prayer rostrum usually found in the center of the orthodox synagogue, had been eliminated. Instead, prayer benches faced an imposing altar from which choir, organ, and cantor conducted decorous, ecumenical ceremonies.[22]

"Change with the spirit of the generation," manifested in liturgical revisions and the internal arrangements of the prayer hall, eventually affected the exterior design of Emanu-El, as well.[23] As early as 1902, an uneasiness with the congregation's ethnocentric emblems, particularly its "Moresque towers," raised demands for revision in accordance with the "inevitable westward trend of

78   Signs of Changes

Progress."[24] Consequently, after the fire and earthquake of 1906 destroyed the old temple, a resurrected house of worship adapted numerous modifications. Whereas the signs of the old structure had emphasized Judaism's uniqueness, the new Emanu-El, constructed on the same Sutter Street site, adjusted its symbolism according to the changing winds of contemporary urban culture. Dedicated in 1907, the structure reflected the growing standardization of San Francisco as it became an integral part of the continental metropolitan network. (Figure 9)

The new structure altered the 1866 balance between ethnocentric cultural emblems and class-oriented architecture. The reconstructed temple was first and foremost, an affluent, yet generic house of worship; no oversized facade declared the denomination of its worshippers. While the general contours of the new temple resembled its predecessor, the rococo entrance and its imposing oriental towers were not rebuilt. The initial impression of the temple, uncluttered with Jewish symbolism and deprived of Moresque turrets, announced the presence of a prosperous, yet ordinary religious sanctuary with little emphasis of its Jewish orientation. Only close scrutiny revealed that the house of worship belonged to Jews.

Construction problems and budgetary constraints influenced the lowering of temple turrets. But, in addition, a radical change in style preferences also affected the new version of the temple towers. "Why should the Jewish people be so proud of ... the old Russian domes?" the temple's Rabbi Voorsanger demanded contentiously.

> Is it characteristic of the Hebrew faith? Surely not. These domes have therefore been replaced by towers, while lower, have decidedly more character for a synagogue than the former ones.[25]

The new towers were not only lower. They also peaked in conical Gothic-style rooftops which were more in tune with contemporary church architecture than the old bulbous domes. Rabbi Voorsanger's harsh characterization of the former turrets as "Russian" suggested a certain uneasiness concerning the tone of Judaism in San Francisco at the turn of the century. By 1907, significant numbers of indigent Eastern European Jews had reached the city. The foreign mannerisms of newcomers prompted the congregation's leaders to reconsider the balance between religious emblems as signs of ethnic identity, and the structure's general architectural conception as a symbol of belonging within a broad American context. Hence, a blunt articulation of affinity with gentile neighbors affected the design of the temple. In addition to the truncated gothic towers, the Tablets of the Law were removed from the apex of the structure and placed at a much lower position. Stars of David were removed from the masonry of the building—turrets and facade included—and appeared in windows only. From a distance, Emanu-El invoked impressions of a vaguely "church" architecture, with only muffled symbols of distinct Jewish roots.

As in the old Sutter Street Temple, the interior arrangements of Emanu-El presaged future moves towards an even stronger adherence with mainstream cultural mores. The temple's prayer hall, adorned with numerous trappings of California architecture, explicitly blended into San Francisco's social and cultural landscape. Potted palm trees, an organic metaphor for California's Hispanic origins, flanked the altar, while exposed pine trusses traversed the ceiling in accordance with the current local vogue of employing mission-style building techniques.[26] In 1923, a new Temple Emanu-El, situated on Lake Street, strengthened the California theme even further. The new temple was a formidable example of popular Spanish-revival architecture. (Figure 10) Both the architectural philosophy and cultural idioms of the 1923 temple departed significantly from those of previous temple structures.

The Temple on Lake Street once again modified the balance between cultural symbols and architecture. The building was distinctly Californian in its design. In fact, the new Emanu-El bore a striking resemblance to the Palace of Liberal Arts at San Francisco's Panama-Pacific Exposition of 1915, which was to become a prototype for ceremonial architecture in California. With its immaculate white-washed walls, and rustic, red-tiled dome, the building represented a perfect example of mission-revival architecture.[27] Only the Tablets of the Law—placed over a main doorway, but within a secluded inner courtyard—meekly announced that the mission building on Lake Street, in actual fact, housed a synagogue. Visually, the temple attempted to blend into the landscape. Emanu-El's design suggested that the temple's function as a peculiarly Californian cultural center bore precedence over distant religious connotations. Its province as a Jewish house of prayer could be ascertained only by furtive glimpses into the courtyard or by actually entering the secluded inner sanctum. The mission-synagogue visibly eradicated foreign, distant elements from

80 Signs of Changes

progressive Judaism. This California temple embodied a tangible common denominator between mainstream society and the city's established Jewry.

Like Emanu-El, the "liberal" Sherith Israel synagogue passed through various stages of revising the balance between ethnic identity and communal affiliations. As in the case of Congregation Emanu-El, Sherith Israel's various edifices were cultural artifacts, reflecting the social conditions of their builders and the historical period in which they were constructed. In the 1870 dedication of its second and most opulent temple, the congregation extolled ties with a Jewish culture which was distinctly non-Californian. Like Emanu-El it also incorporated minarets, corpulent Stars of David, and the Tablets of the Law over the main gable. (Figure 11) Yet, when the facade was renovated during the late 1890s, important changes occurred. Although the minarets remained quite ornate, the main entrance was remodeled in a more conventional gothic style, and the magnanimous Star of David over the main entrance diminished significantly in size. Sherith Israel appeared to be moving towards compliance with mainstream religious architecture. (Figure 12) During the late nineteenth century Sherith Israel's parishioners sought gentrification and de-semiticization of their liturgy, too. Already in the 1880s, worshippers objected to the "sobbing" of a cantor who sang according to orthodox traditions. Families sat together in Sherith Israel's prayer hall without distinctions of gender. Sermons were conducted in English.[28]

Conformity through structural design had an even more apparent effect on Sherith Israel's new temple, dedicated in 1905. Its dome, a fashionable architectural element in early twentieth-century San Francisco churches, stressed common values between the religion practiced within the confines of the building and its immediate California surroundings. (Figure 13) "No sane person will entertain the thought that we must shape our houses of worship in an Oriental style, or that Judaism finds a more fitting, visible expression in Moorish art or Byzantine mode of architecture," stated the rabbi of Sherith Israel.[29] Looking over his shoulder at the rival Sutter Street temple of Congregation Emanu-El and its indiscriminate blending of styles, "the combination of Romanesque - Gothic - Episcopal architecture," Rabbi Jacob Nieto called for a standardizied synagogue architecture "in accordance with modern ideas." In his temple the rabbi saw an ideal fusion of the unique and the traditional. The large dome of Sherith Israel conveyed a dignified "lofty" presentation of Judaism, "yet without any attempt at scraping the sky." Oriental color schemes and explicit symbols of Judaism appeared primarily within the secluded confines of the central prayer hall.[30]

Ron Robin

In contrast to the revisionist Sherith Israel and Emanu-El, the more traditional congregations of Ohabei Shalom and Beth Israel resisted the use of architecture as counterpoise to the ethnocentricity of religious emblems. When the members of Ohabei Shalom built a new house of worship in 1894, they relied heavily on Moresque architecture. In fact the structure resembled a mosque more than a synagogue. (Figure 14) Nevertheless, the internal arrangement of prayer halls at the two traditional synagogues suggested that their differences with progressive Judaism were semantic rather than substantive. While professing "no change or alteration from the ancient rituals," the venerable Beth Israel accepted the use of musical instruments in its prayer sessions, adopted the system of family pews, and discarded the centrally placed Bimah for an "altar" in its temple built in 1891.[31] The two traditional congregations preferred muted manifestations of integration, and agreed that inscrutable and foreign rituals should be modified. "So many lies are manufactured about us," the rabbi of Ohabei Shalom noted in the 1880s,

> and they gain credence among the unthinking and the ignorant.... Throw open the doors and let people view us as we are. In this way we dissolve antipathies and make friendships, and when efforts are made to defame us, we will have friends who will champion the truth.[32]

With this dictum in mind, San Francisco's Jewish press, traditional and reform, pounced upon every opportunity to prove that Jews, despite obvious differences, were typically American in their behavior. Portraying Jews as historical American stereotypes was the most common mode of identifying Judaism as being unquestionably American. In fact, occasional boosters even speculated that the ultimate Americans, the Indians, were of Hebrew origin. If this appeared somewhat speculative, the Jewish press insisted that Jews had "already sown the seeds of civilization" in the Americas long before the arrival of the Pilgrims.[33]

On the front page of Emanu-El's commemorative edition celebrating 250 years of Jewish presence in America, a picture of "Peter Stuyvesant ... watching the landing of the first Jewish colonists in the United States [Sic]." reiterated the Jew's claim for legitimacy in the New World.[34] Even Columbus was a Jew, a local community figure informed an eager audience. As for the Civil War, the ultimate

82 Signs of Changes

test of loyalty, Jews proved themselves by giving a "larger proportion of their sons to the union than [did] any other denomination."[35]

In accordance with the changing architecture of local synagogues, the Jewish press increasingly narrowed its focus so as to present Jews as not only American in their behavior, but typically Californian, too. Occasionally, when a Jew managed to make a local college football team, the Jewish media interpreted this phenomenon as a sign of Judaism's compatibility with local society. According to a typical comment, "the Jewish youth upon the gridiron challenged those who accused Jews of being foreign to the soil of California."[36]

Early editions of the local Jewish press had emphasized the unique economic acumen and business skills of co-religionists in the Golden State. By the turn of the century, and in accordance with popular disaffection with mavericks of the gold rush period, a typically American image of Jews emerged. Instead of businessmen, they appeared as "the puritans of the western states"; not an irresponsible, "screaming roaring element" but a community of "builders who quietly and without glory pursued their labors."[37] Jews were not a nation of shopkeepers, but pioneers driving ox teams over the plains, braving "deserts and floods, the raids of Indians and the attacks of desperados," all for "the ulterior object of establishing permanent homes" and families. The success of Jews in San Francisco was not attributed to business skills but to the geographic latitudes of northern California which were the same as those of Palestine, the fountainhead of Judaism. The sons of ancient Hebrews succeeded because instinctively they felt they were re-creating the Promised Land in California.[38]

The re-writing of Jewish history in California complemented the changing morphology of synagogue architecture in the city. By hallowing the portable elements of a transplanted heritage rather than its immutable customs, architectural and historical revisionism strengthened Jewish identity without rocking the urban boat. Both reformists and traditionalists encouraged familiarity with Judaism through modification of religious symbols. Opening the doors of Judaism to public scrutiny was also a central motif of the local Jewish press, particularly in its enthusiastic reporting on Jewish presence—real or fabricated—in local historical events. Established Jews had thrived financially and spiritually in the fickle urban climate of San Francisco because they had adjusted to local circumstances. When gentile neighbors glanced at the Jewish press or studied their temples, they saw a people who could be different and yet the same.

Ron Robin   83

Beyond their exclusively Jewish context, both the Jewish press and communal architecture revealed an important aspect of urban culture in general. In the days of the boom-town mentality, San Francisco's Jews had regarded themselves as an individual entity in search of private and personal satisfaction. Their temples were mostly personal monuments in a private city. The intrusion of an incipient market system on the urban texture led local Jews, like other segments of San Francisco's economic elite, to define themselves according to class, whether through ostentatious temples, or participation in elitist pastimes, such as collegiate football. By the late nineteenth century there came an awareness of the mutual dependencies which characterized the capitalist economic network of turn-of-the-century America. This particular phase produced a wave of pseudo-indigenous communal architecture as well as the characterization of Jews as typical Californians in community newsletters. By the early twentieth century San Francisco's Jews articulated their identity, according to conventional standards, much like their gentile peers and contemporaries. To a large degree they had internalized the "other directedness" which was typical of Modern America's urban culture. Their definition of self in the early twentieth century reflected what Gunther Barth has called Metropolism, the tendency to foster certain class-transcending, common modes of urban behavior throughout the continental urban network and irrespective of geographical location.[39]

This concept of metropolitan culture which was prevalent among San Francisco's established Jewry appears to have been challenged in the waning years of the nineteenth century. Beginning in the late 1880s and shrouded in a mantle of cultural inscrutability, small numbers of eastern European Jews slowly drifted towards the Bay Area. Primarily Russians, Poles, and Rumanians, these impoverished Hebrew immigrants were the children of a beleaguered Jewish culture, the victims of acute economic deprivation, and vicious anti-Semitism.[40] Most hailed from the confines of Russia's Jewish Pale of Settlement. This huge territorial ghetto, which encompassed most of Poland, Lithuania, Byelorussia, and the Ukraine, was the creation of a Tsarist autocracy beset by religious scruples and folk fears of the Jew. Forced to live in homogeneous enclaves, and isolated from the winds of intellectual change, the Jews of the Pale produced a culture based exclusively on Jewish traditions and religion. In Galicia, Rumania, and other areas of Jewish concentration, the situation differed only in degree, not in kind. Throughout eastern Europe Jews were treated as a separate national group, and they acted accordingly. Unlike German Jews who lived in a nationally

84

homogeneous but religiously diverse society, eastern European Jews were one element among many in a multi-cultural milieu in which religion and nationality intimately intertwined. Tsarist rulers were Russian Orthodox, Polish neighbors were Roman Catholic, and Jews could not avoid identifying their religion with an insular sense of nationality.

Within this context, religious reform was superfluous. No modification of tradition could open up new avenues for a people marked with a stigma of religion and race. One either embraced traditional religion or, as the Tsarist world began to crumble, sought salvation in socialism. Class differences, the result of restrictions on movement and occupation, also distinguished eastern European Jews from the previous wave of Hebrew migration to the United States. Like their German co-religionists, they had occupied the ranks of shopkeepers, money lenders, and other service professions. However, with the emancipation of serfs in 1863 and the transition from a medieval economy to gradual industrialization, the traditional role of Jews as economic middlemen in a stagnant eastern European society fell by the wayside. Jewish villages, unable to support a growing population in a decaying economic environment, spewed millions of their inhabitants into the unknown city. Blocked access to urban professions, restraints on ownership of land, and the demise of crafts and trades turned petty merchants and skilled artisans into an urban proletariat. Redundant and outmoded skills propelled Jews to the ranks of semi-skilled and unskilled laborers. Continuous economic flux, coupled with periodic outbursts of violent anti-Semitism, sparked widespread interest in emigration to the United States where, rumor had it, work and tolerance abounded.

In America, class discrepancies, diametrically opposed religious beliefs, and divergent concepts of nationality set newcomers apart from their established peers. The Jewish establishment feared the presence of an impoverished proletariat bound by stagnant religious piety or, conversely, espousing a frightening political radicalism. From the shores of San Francisco Bay, the outspoken Rabbi Voorsanger warned that "our homogeneity with these people" had long ceased to exist. "The national and domestic environment of these people are not ours" he cautioned; "their language, their mode of life, their habits, and even their religious conceptions are not ours."[41] Most of Voorsanger's disowned cousins conveniently remained along the eastern seaboard. Nevertheless, anxiety levels in the Bay Area remained high. Observing the arrival of impoverished brethren at the turn of the century, the city's established Jewry saw child-like masses, prattling in a "nauseating ... Jew Jargon," clinging to an "unpalatable Judaism," while gregariously huddling in a crowded ghetto, a "Russia transplanted to California."[42] Impending immigration routes to the west coast through the Panama Canal fueled foreboding of a "foreign city" within the city of San Francisco. "Anyone who wants to see Polish and Russian Jews without going to that knouted, plague-stricken country," a prominent member of San Francisco's Jewish establishment lashed out, "can have the whole outfit on the lower levels of Folsom and Howard streets" in the city's working class district.[43]

Already, in 1895, a Jewish socialist club appeared on the scene. Trepidations heightened even further at the spectacle of agnostic Russian Jews "creating an Irish disturbance" while feasting at a restaurant on Yom Kippur, a day of fasting and mourning observed even by Reform Jews. Blatant contempt for religion was as disturbing as the curious rituals of "pseudo-orthodoxy" with its "muezzin" for a rabbi, and its "reader, a howling dervish."[44] In lieu of dignified Reform rabbis as community leaders, the spiritual sages of newcomers worshipped in storefront synagogues, eking out a living as petty traders or junk dealers.[45]

Salvaging the Jewish image in San Francisco, therefore, demanded sharp reactions from the establishment's uplifters. Counteracting specters of ghetto life in San Francisco followed predictable patterns. Community sponsored Settlement Houses offered "not an additional institution for the fostering of pauperism," but "the elevation of the poor to a stage of self-reliance."[46] A Jewish Educational Society waged war against the seeds of socialism and anarchism by inculcating the finer points of Judaism to the "children of the proletariat."[47] San Francisco's Hebrew Board of Relief sought a modicum of control over the flow of immigrants to the city through tight control of relief aid, while community organizations funded back-to-the-land projects for the benefit of newcomers.[48] As in the east, factions within the established community sought radical solutions not through aid, but by means of immigration restriction. Led by Temple Emanu-El's Rabbi Voorsanger, vocal choruses demanded strict curtailment of Jewish immigration. "We have shielded and protected the Russian brother and he has created problems that we find difficult to solve," Emanu-El's prelate proclaimed in justification of his anti-immigration stance.[49] Local opponents joined Jewish restrictionists throughout the country in pointing accusing fingers at the reclusiveness of newcomers and the prohibitive costs of often futile attempts to Americanize Jewish immigrants. Even the funding of agricultural projects, which promised to dilute Jewish concentrations in San Francisco, were denounced as

86 Signs of Changes

being both expensive and unrealistic, because "fundamentally, the Jew is city bred."[50]

The clamorings of restrictionists in San Francisco bore no relationship to reality. By all accounts, anti-Semitism in the city was marginal, almost non-existent.[51] In addition, newcomers from eastern Europe did not reach San Francisco in overwhelming numbers. In 1910, only 5,254 were counted by the census bureau.[52] While estimates of a deluge of newcomers flowing through the almost completed Panama Canal might have fanned restrictionist sentiment, the uncompromising stand of Jewish immigration foes in San Francisco was compounded by an inability to comprehend the cultural standards of newcomers. Affluent veterans misconstrued the life patterns of Jewish immigrants in the city. Occasional uplifters recognized the potential embedded in Jewish working class quarters. Yet, the absence of flourishing fields arranged in familiar, middle class fashion intimated that newcomers belonged to another world and were doomed to repeat the embarrassing behavior of ghetto dwellers in eastern cities.

San Francisco's established Jewry looked on helplessly as their "co-religionists" transgressed standards of genteel behavior. The involvement of newcomers in urban politics was particularly disconcerting as pleas to avoid mixing politics with religion fell on empty ears. To the great disappointment of established community leaders, tiny orthodox congregations became obligatory campaign stops for vote seekers. When a candidate for mayor complained that the Jewish vote was being manipulated against him, a nebulous reply in the newsletter of the establishment congregation, *Emanu-El*, suggested that the veteran Jewish community was completely unaware who had chastised him and why. "There is no such thing as a Jewish vote," the periodical claimed, and even if hasty words had been uttered somewhere, by someone, nobody, the paper unconvincingly stated, controlled Jewish political behavior.[53] In the eyes of established Jewry, bartering votes was the epitome of a bovine and dangerous ghetto mentality which seemed to be on the upsurge in San Francisco. Repugnant ward politics also questioned the continuing existence of a flexible but genteel code of conduct in San Francisco. Difficulties in identifying acknowledged immigrant leaders complicated attempts to enlighten newcomers. An anxious Voorsanger exhorted his newly arrived co-religionists to look up to their rabbis as leaders and masters, but to no avail.[54] In accordance with the traditions of eastern Europe, most orthodox congregations did not have permanent leaders;

Ron Robin   87

none treated their rabbis as leaders. The rabbis of eastern Europe were professional experts on Jewish law, not community leaders.[55]

Despite the misgivings of uptown Jews, the immigrants' concept of culture was not diametrically opposed to that of their established peers. Newcomers' involvement in municipal politics was a symptom of swift acclimatization, a benchmark on the road of rapid Americanization rather than a perpetuation of ghetto life. The absence of tight communal frameworks catalyzed, rather than delayed, familiarity with local urban mores. In fact, a homogeneous Jewish district—the epitome of un-American life styles—never materialized in San Francisco's working class districts. Within the setting of heterogeneous immigrant neighborhoods, the rituals of Jewish newcomers proved to be as susceptible to change as had been the elegant adornments of uptown temples.

Before the fire and earthquake of 1906, most indigent Jews resided south of Market Street, in a tenement district bounded by Mission and Harrison streets, from Fourth Street as far as Eleventh.[56] It was not an exclusive ethnic neighborhood; among Jewish families, one could find a host of other European immigrant groups. No concentrated residential patterns of Jews ever developed around any industrial concentrations either, because Jews never dominated specific industries, as they did the garment trade in New York's lower east side. In addition, Jewish immigrants, who invariably came to the city with families, spread throughout low income neighborhoods, seeking suitable accommodation for comparatively large households. Thus, they avoided the typical initial stage of ethnic migration: tight, overcrowded concentration of young single males, living and working in close quarters.

An intimate Jewish neighborhood—not a ghetto—did eventually materialize in the aftermath of the fire and earthquake of 1906. Approximately five hundred of San Francisco's poorest Jewish families joined a small cluster of their brethren on the distant southern outskirts of the city, in the vicinity of San Bruno Road, between Felton and Silliman streets. There, a collection of Jewish "carpenters, smiths, and masons, tailors and factory hands, hucksters, peddlers, and petty traders" formed a loosely- knit Jewish community.[57] Despite the neighborhood's Jewish flavor, it did not have about it the aura of a crowded urban ghetto. A glance at contemporary insurance maps reveal thinly settled, unpaved streets of frame dwellings, mostly renovated refugee cottages from the fire and earthquake, laced among open fields, and surrounded by flower nurseries and truck farms.[58] Insular ethnicity associated with east coast ghettoes did not thrive "out the road"

88   Signs of Changes

as the neighborhood was known. Many Jewish newcomers had arrived in the city
as seasoned veterans of metropolitan life, having undergone the rites of passage
to a multi-cultural climate in other American cities.[59] In addition, Italian truck
farmers and Portuguese gardeners residing in the neighborhood endowed the area
with a freeflowing cosmopolitan complexion.

As was the case in the South-of-Market district before 1906, the working
milieu of San Bruno Road's Jews also failed to produce alternate frameworks for
group solidarity. Unlike their Italian and Portuguese neighbors who worked in
surrounding truck gardens, no industry invited an exclusive garnering of Jews. A
large segment of San Bruno Road's Hebrews lived the lives of itinerant peddlers
and junk dealers, roaming the streets of San Francisco, perhaps bringing back to
their neighborhoods enticing aromas of the metropolis.

Although a vocal minority of newcomers adhered strictly to the traditions
of their forefathers, most Jews "out the road" were only nominally orthodox.[60]
Their orthodox background had probably been more the result of cultural inertia
in their native lands than religious piety. In this sense, concepts of culture among
the Jews of the San Bruno neighborhood resembled that of their affluent
predecessors in the city who had turned to their religious institutions as a means
of displaying a figurative cultural creed. The kind of values retained among San
Brunoities were those that invoked a comparison between past experience and
immediate perception, those that clarified the issues concerning them most
persistently.

The articulation of culture among Jews along San Bruno road should not
be sought in the architecture of their synagogues. To be sure, synagogues existed,
but they did not fulfill the same function of uptown temples. Tucked in among
neighborhood streets stood two large synagogues, lacking in heat, electrical lights,
and—in accordance with orthodox custom—a definitive leadership.[61] Unlike the
houses of worship of affluent peers, poor economic conditions precluded cultural
expression through the physical features of immigrant synagogues. Under these
circumstances, newcomers, both in San Bruno and in other concentrations of
working class Jews within the city, expressed their concepts of culture through
modification of religious rituals.

Religious practices took on contemporary symbolic meanings in the
synagogues of the San Bruno Road area. For the most part, gestures of piety
were retained, but their original meanings diminished in significance. Within the
synagogues, worshippers observed traditional modes of prayer, but not their

original content. Immigrants retained "instruction in how to perform their duties as a Jew, but they didn't know why," nor did they seem to care.[62] Jewish holidays, as visible opportunities to reassert adherence to the faith, were primarily communal events, the dogmatic significance of which aroused sparse interest. Along San Bruno road, Jews faithfully observed the colorful decorum surrounding Passover celebrations, the carnival atmosphere of Purim, and the solemn soul-searching of Yom Kippur. But, when neighborhood children inquired about the significance of their heritage and traditions, their elders could only "tell you things from the Talmud in Yiddish, various proverbs, and little stories" meant to salvage the significance of the holidays in a transplanted environment. Like the celebration of Columbus Day by Italian neighbors and the enthusiastic participation of Hispanics in San Francisco's Portola pageantry, colorful Jewish holidays, reduced to the level of folk religion, asserted an identity which did not contradict cultural acclimatization.[63] In their simplified versions, even non-Jewish neighbors could participate in Jewish celebrations.[64] Thus, a modified acceptance of arcane traditions enabled Jewish newcomers to stabilize links to the present and blend into contemporary concepts of the future.

Traditional meals provided another tangible forum for expressing selective adherence to the faith. Familiar aromas of traditional dishes enveloped the entire neighborhood during the high holidays and on the Sabbath. Nevertheless, the rules of Kashruth, the stringent dietary rules governing the Jewish kitchen, never commanded suchlike adherence. Often, with the demise of grandparents, dietary restrictions passed away, too.[65]

Asserting identity through highly visible folk customs was accompanied by the abandoning of complex and personally restraining traditions. Along with Kashruth, the strict observance of the Sabbath declined. On Saturdays Jewish stores in San Francisco's working-class districts usually closed their doors "until about 1910 or 1912, and then, of course, you kept it open."[66] Many breadwinners in the San Bruno Road area were independent peddlers or petty merchants. Consequently, the decision to work on Saturdays was probably one of individual choice, not an unconditional capitulation to the forces of industrial life.

Language retention, and its associations with an insular Jewish culture, was also jettisoned. Even pious newcomers neglected Hebrew, the language of the Scriptures. Yiddish, the heart and soul of eastern European Jewish culture, did not fare well either. "They used to call me 'the little kike' when I'd go to [my]... uncle's house because I spoke Yiddish," a resident of the San Bruno

90   Signs of Changes

neighborhood remembered.[67] Neither a struggling Yiddish newspaper, nor travelling Yiddish theaters affected predominant sentiments that "we're too far out west to speak Yiddish."[68] Like the refashioning of cultural icons on the temples of uptown Jews, transitions in language loyalties among San Bruno Road's Jews signaled a willingness to abandon seemingly superficial differences between newcomers and mainstream society. Growing up in San Francisco, the scions of working class immigrants recalled parents attending English language night schools, communal readings of newspapers and English books on street corners, as well as exposure to the distinctly American rags-to-riches stories of Horatio Alger and Frank Merriwell.[69]

As patterns of an opaque culture were relinquished, subterfuges emerged to fill the ensuing vacuum. At the bustling corner of San Bruno and Burrows roads stood the Emanu-El Sisterhood settlement house; across the street lay the imposing Avenue Theater Nickelodeon.[70] Both establishments complemented modified Jewish traditions by providing additional sources of identity and guidance. A visit to the movies was a weekly event even among poor families. Through the heroes of the silent screen, young immigrants participated vicariously in the triumphs and failures of American life. Both dime novels and nickelodeons bolstered a sense of orientation among newcomers. Even the poorest of dramas, Jane Addams observed, brought "cause and effect, will power and action, once more into relationship and gives a man a thrilling conviction that he may yet be master of his fate."[71] Movies and urban adventure novelettes restored a semblance of order to the "bewildering facts of life" by convincing viewers that, with a little bit of luck and a strong commitment to practical versatility, they could still control their lives.[72]

Helping immigrants adjust to modern America and "western ideas of culture" was also the initial task of the neighborhood's settlement house.[73] Organized activities, run by uptown Jews from Temple Emanu-El, focused on the teaching of urban etiquette, although frequenters of the settlement house often sidestepped any patronizing undertones. Not the condescending attitudes of social workers, but "the beautiful things that most of us didn't have at home,"—books, attractive furniture, flowers and plants—beckoned residents of the San Bruno Road neighborhood to the corner of Burrows Road.[74] Indeed, an intense scrutinizing of immigrant behavior in the San Bruno area soon convinced uptown Jews that Americanization was somehow taking care of itself. "Who reminds a person who dips his body in a cask of scarlet dye to take on a scarlet

Ron Robin 91

hue?" To be an American, according to this typical observation, "is to move on the line of least resistance."[75] Close contact with newcomers through the settlement house eventually provided even the shrillest of restrictionists with a new found empathy for upstarts and their "strikingly rapid assimilation ... with the spirit of the country."[76]

Although they were reluctant to recall their modest beginnings, a similarity of fortunes existed between middle class benefactors and impoverished brethren. In the 1850s, San Francisco's squalid Central Wharf district, known as the Jew's Quarter, was inundated with "Jew slopsellers."[77] Their ragged appearances and vigorous hawking provoked comments about "oxed-eyed, cunning oily Jews," and invited discrimination by credit agencies and business interests.[78] A mere twenty years later, many of the same individuals appeared as pillars of strength in San Francisco. At the turn of the century, "bedraggled and unkempt" Jewish newcomers crowded into similar quarters, their "rookeries wedged in between saloons, eating houses, and sailor boarding houses." Based on the experience of their established peers, few doubted that within a few years they would "move uptown" and "take their place in the community as self-respecting" citizens.[79] Like uptown Jews, newcomers distilled the portable aspects of their religion. As such, they signaled that, like those who preceded them, they too could establish an acceptable balance between the unique qualities of their faith and the demands of urban life.

If anything, San Francisco's established Jewry expressed alarm at what they perceived as a total abandoning of Jewish roots by eastern European newcomers and an overheated process of Americanization. Accordingly, benefactors fostered through settlement programs a selective and cautious revival of elements of an eastern European culture which they had previously condemned. The settlement house's religious schools provided instruction in Yiddish for immigrant offspring who experienced difficulties in communicating with old-world parents and grandparents. In addition, Temple Emanu-El offered financial assistance to struggling Orthodox synagogues in the San Bruno neighborhood.[80]

A full circle had been accomplished with the transition of settlement houses from missionaries to havens of an indigenous culture. Despite obvious differences in style, San Francisco's established Jews acknowledged that newcomers responded to urban life in a manner similar to their own. Both newcomers and veterans felt that the inner qualities of their culture would best survive by establishing a reputation as flexible participants in urban life. Perhaps the most

92 Signs of Changes

indicative sign of a meeting of minds occurred with the 1915 inauguration of an orthodox synagogue, Knesseth Israel, in the working class district along Golden Gate Avenue. Despite its orthodox orientation, officers of the synagogue decided on what they called the "Mission Style" for the edifice.[81] Quaint red-tiled roofs and the gleaming white walls of the Spanish revival style removed any doubts as to stubborn adherence to orthodoxy within the synagogue. The predominance of fluid frontiers in San Francisco—social, economic, and physical—and the city's frequent process of rebuilding, encouraged strikingly similar forms of visible cultural adaptation among newcomers and veterans, Jews and gentiles. As symbolically displayed in the rapid reproduction of Mission-synagogues, Jews blunted their differences with other city people by emphasizing a shared taste for pseudo-indigenous architecture, a vague affinity with a mythical past of which almost no San Franciscans had been part.

Judaism in San Francisco, even among the orthodox was not an immutable creed, but a tool for making sense of life in an urban whirl. The introduction of mission architecture in immigrant synagogues signalled that newcomers, like their affluent predecessors, intended to use their culture to achieve the good life. Changing architectural styles in San Francisco's temples and the modification of ritual demonstrated that Jews—immigrants and veterans—were part and parcel of the fluid, versatile, and practical American city. The culture of Jews in San Francisco focused on a sense of tradition which did not entail the disruption of an everyday American routine. Their signs of ethnicity were cleansed of the complexity of what appeared to be anachronistic, irrelevant origins. San Francisco's Jews, according to the formula articulated by Herbert Gans, created an ethnicity of signs rather than binding content.[82] They had formulated a culture which in no way interfered with their pragmatic responses to the imperatives of their roles and positions in American society at large.

Figure 8
Temple Emanu-El, Sutter Street, Dedicated 1866.
(Courtesy, Bancroft Library, University of California)

Figure 9
Temple Emanu-El, Sutter Street,
Reconstructed after Earthquake of 1906.
(Courtesy of Bancroft Library, University of California)

Figure 10
Temple Emanu-El, Lake Street, 1923.
(Photograph by Marlene Getz)

Figure 11
Congregation Sherith Israel, 1870.
Temple Emanu-El appears in the Background.
(Courtesy, Bancroft Library, University of California)

Figure 12
Congregation Sherith Israel after Refurbishing, circa 1900.
(Courtesy, Bancroft Library, University of California)

Figure 13
The New Sherith Israel, 1905.
(From: Western Press Association, *Modern San Francisco, 1907-1908*)

Figure 14
Congregation Ohabei Shalome, 1894.
(From: Western Press Association, *Modern San Francisco, 1907-1908*)

Notes

1. Harvey Rice, *Letters From the Pacific Slope or; First Impressions* (New York, 1870), 67-68, 77-79; Frank Le Couvreur, *From East Prussia to the Golden Gate* (New York, 1906), 174-176.
2. Rice, *Letters From the Pacific Slope*, 78; Jacob Voorsanger, *The Chronicles of Emanu-El* (San Francisco, 1900), 114. The architectural significance of this particular version of Temple Emanu-El is discussed in Allan Temko, "Temple Emanu-El of San Francisco; a Glory of the West," *Commentary*, 26 (August, 1958),117; Harold Kirker, *California's Architectural Frontier; Style and Tradition in the Nineteenth Century* (San Marino, Ca., 1960),76.
3. Over the years the Jews of Posen have been labeled as Poles even though the province fell into Prussian hands in 1772 and its Jewish inhabitants spoke German. See Fred Rosenbaum, *Architects of Reform; Congregational and Community Leadership, Emanu-El of San Francisco, 1849-1980* (Berkeley, 1980), 1-2.
4. An example of Jewish peddlers in the far west is discussed in Gunther Barth, *Instant Cities* (New York, 1975), 72-73.
5. The following overview of German Jews and Reform is based on Nathan Glazer, *American Judaism* (Chicago, 1972), 22-42.
6. On the relationship between Reform Judaism and Americanization see Leon A. Jick, *The Americanization of the Synagogue, 1820-1870* (Hanover, N. H., 1976).
7. Marc Lee Raphael, "Rabbi Jacob Voorsanger of San Francisco on Jews and Judaism; the Implications of the Pittsburgh Platform," *American Jewish Historical Quarterly*, 63 (December,1973), 185-207.
8. *Ibid.*
9. Peter R. Decker, *Fortunes and Failures; White Collar Mobility in Nineteenth Century San Francisco* (Cambridge, Mass., 1978), 96-97, 81.
10. *Ibid.*, 82; Rudolph Glanz, *The Jews of California, From the Discovery of Gold Until 1880* (New York, 1960), 5.
11. For an overview of the Jewish establishment's congregations see Michael Zarchin, *Glimpses of Jewish Life in San Francisco* (Oakland, Ca., 1964), 81-100.
12. Rice, *Letter From the Pacific Slope*, 78.
13. Voorsanger, *Chronicles of Emanu-El*, 114.

14. *Emanu-El*, November 22, 1895.
15. *Ibid.*, March 2, 1906, 14.
16. San Francisco *Call*, April 6, 1895, 14.
17. For a description of a typical union service see *Emanu-El*, December 8, 1911, 8-9.
18. Jacob Voorsanger, *Ritual for Friday Evening Service* (San Francisco, N. D.).
19. S. Homer Henley, "Yom Kippur in Temple Emanu-El, 1896" (Ms., Western Jewish Historical Center, Berkeley). In the Following footnotes the center will be denoted as WJHC.
20. San Francisco *Examiner*, October 12, 1913, 43.
21. *Ibid.*, October 11, 1913, 6.
22. Voorsanger, *Chronicles of Emanu-El*, 47, illustration opposite page 112.
23. *Emanu-El*, November 22, 1895, 5.
24. *Examiner* cited in Emanu-El, October 31, 1902, 7.
25. *Emanu-El*, March 29, 1907, 10; September 6, 1907, 11.
26. *Ibid.*, illustration on page 7.
27. *The Blue Book; a Comprehensive Official Souvenir View Book of the Panama-Pacific International Exposition at San Francisco, 1915* (San Francisco, 1915), 87, 97. Within this context see also Rachel Wischnitzer, *Synagogue Architecture in the United States* (Philadelphia, 1955), 117. Note that Wiscchnitzer misidentified the building as resembling the Panama-Pacific building at the San Diego Exposition due to a misreading of photo captions in her reference sources.
28. Harriet Lane Levy, *920 O'Farrell Street* (New York, 1937), 91-92, 235-236. See also Jacob Nieto, *Sabbath Eve Service and Hymns and Anthems for Sabbath and Holidays Compiled for Congregation Sherith Israel* (San Francisco, 1899).
29. *Jewish Times and Observer*, March 15, 1912, 12. Although the article was not signed, the pugnacious writing style is that of Rabbi Jacob Nieto of Sherith Israel who was temporary editor of the paper at the time.
30. *Ibid.*; *Emanu-El*, September 29, 1905, 54.
31. *Emanu-El*, March 29, 1907, 8; *Jewish Times and Observer*, September 25, 1908, 5 and October 2, 1908, 1.
32. Rabbi A. S. Bettleheim cited in the autobiography of his daughter, Rebekah Kohut, *My Portion* (New York, 1925), 34-55.
33. *Jewish Times and Observer*, October 4, 1912, 10; *Emanu-El*, April 4, 1905, 6.

102 Signs of Changes

34. *Emanu-El*, September 29, 1905, front cover.

35. *Ibid.*, November 28, 1913, 11.

36. *Ibid.*, December 30, 1904, 8; *Jewish Times and Observer*, November 6, 1914, 7.

37. Rabbi Bernard Kaplan cited in *Emanu-El*, January 6, 1905, ii; Voorsanger cited in *Emanu-El*, June 15, 1906, 2-3.

38. Voorsanger, *Chronicles of Emanu-El*, 14; *Ibid.*, October 13, 1905, 5. See also Bernard Kaplan, "The Jews in America," *Ibid.*, September 29, 1905, 18-20; Lucius Solomon cited in *Ibid.*, April 15, 1915, 4.

39. Gunther Barth, *City People; The Rise of Modern City Culture in Nineteenth-Century America* (New York, 1980), 26.

40. The following description of Jewish Life in eastern Europe is derived from Moses Rischin, *The Promised City; New York Jews 1870-1914* (New York, 1970), 19-33 and Nathan Glazer, *American Judaism* (Chicago, 1972), 60-78.

41. Voorsanger cited in *Emanu-El*, October 24, 1902, 6-7.

42. *Emanu-El*, December 27, 1895, 6, January 20, 1905, 5-6, October 4, 1907, 2; *Call*, April 5, 1897, 7; *Public Opinion*, May 21, 1898, 1.

43. *Public Opinion*, August 13, 1892, 2; *Emanu-El*, January 20, 1905, 5-6.

44. *Emanu-El*, December 6, 1895, 6, December 20, 1895, 5; *Public Opinion*, October 1, 1898, 1.

45. For an example of a Rabbi-junk dealer see Abraham J. Block, "A Family Migration" (Ms., WJHC), 10-12. For an example of an orthodox rabbi who doubled as a petty merchant see advertisement of wares sold by Rabbi Eliahu Berman in *Emanu-El*, April 20, 1909, 3.

46. Emanu-El Sisterhood, *Second Annual Report, 1895-1896* (San Francisco, N.D.), 7, 10. See also *Emanu-El*, November 14, 1913, 2.

47. Zarchin, *Glimpses of Jewish Life in San Francisco*, 168; *Call*, April 5, 1897, 7.

48. See the correspondence between the New York based Industrial Relief Office and the Hebrew Board of Relief in San Francisco (WJHC). The settling of Jews in rural areas is articulated in "The International Society for the Colonization of Russian Jews" (Ms., Bancroft Library, 1891?).

49. *Emanu-El*, February 4, 1898, 8. See also *Ibid.*, January 21, 1898, 5; September 26, 1902, 5-7, January 20, 1905, 5-6.

50. *Ibid.*, January 20, 1905, 6. East Coast reactions to the influx of newcomers is the subject of Sheldon Neuringer, *American Jewry and United States Immigration policy, 1881-1952* (New York, 1980).

Ron Robin   103

51. On the relative lack of anti-semitism in the city see Bernard Kaplan, " The Golden Possibilities of California, " *Emanu-El*, June 21, 1912.

52. United States Bureau of Census, *Thirteenth National Census, 1910*, 6 (Washington, D.C., 1913), 1014.

53. *Emanu-El*, October 9, 1896, 5.

54. Attitudes towards politics among the German Jewish establishment are discussed in Gustav Adolph Danzinger, "The Jews of San Francisco; the Last Half Century," *Overland Monthly*, 25 (April 1895), 398-399. For examples of Orthodox Jews involvement in politics see *Emanu-El*, November 11, 1898, 5; November 7, 1902, 5; *Jewish Times and Observer*, November 1, 1907, 9, November 5, 1909, 10.

55. Interview with Jean Braverman La Pove (Ms., WJHC), 17-18. On the differences between reform rabbis and the traditional approach to rabbinical authority see comments by Marcus Rosenthal, *Emanu-El*, February 24, 1905, 6-9.

56. *Emanu-El*, September 13, 1907, 3.

57. *Ibid.*; Peggy A. Isaak, "How It Was Growing Up 'Out The Road,' "*Jewish Bulletin*, November 19, 1976, 8.

58. Sanborn Map Company, *Insurance Maps of San Francisco* (San Francisco, 1913), vol. 8, 9; Interview with Braverman La Pove, 1; "Oh, It Was a Lovely Life! Lilian Cherney's Recollections of San Francisco, 1900-1940" (Ms., WJHC), 50; Andrew Neustadt, "San Bruno Avenue, The Road" (Ms., WJHC); Steven Liebo, "Out The Road; The San Bruno Avenue Jewish Community of San Francisco, 1901-1968," *Western States Jewish Historical Quarterly* (June, 1979), 99-110.

59. Interview with Braverman La Pove, 6, 31; Interview with Judith Goldfarb (Ms., WJHC), 3.

60. On ultra-orthodox Jews in the San Bruno Road neighborhood see *Jewish Times and Observer*, January 5, 1912, 3. The concept of nominal orthodoxy was first suggested in a seminal article by Charles Liebman, "Orthodoxy in American Jewish Life," *American Jewish Yearbook*, 66 (New York, 1965), 21-95.

61. *Insurance Maps of San Francisco*, Vol. 8; Interview with Viviane Dudune Solomon (Ms., WJHC), 9; Interview with Braverman La Pove, 17-18.

62. Interview with Dudune Solomon, 6.

104 Signs of Changes

63. Interview with Braverman-La Pove, 10-11, 43; On the subject of symbolic celebration of Jewish rites see: Herbert Gans, "Symbolic Ethnicity; The Future of Ethnic Groups," in Herbert Gans (ed.), *On the Making of Americans; Essays in Honor of David Riesman* (Pittsburg, Pa., 1979), 193-220.

64. Interview with Dudune Solomon, 25.

65. Interview with Braverman La Pove, 10-11; Interview with Rose Hartman Ets-Hokin (Ms., WJHC), 6; "Oh, What a Beautiful Life," 3.

66. "Oh, What a Beautiful Life," 3.

67. *Ibid.*, 26; Interview with Dudune Solomon, 6, 8.

68. "Oh What a Beautiful Life," 26; Interview with Jesse Levin (Ms., WJHC), 12-14.

69. *Ibid.*; Interview with Reuben Waxman (Ms., WJHC), 4, 7, 58; Interview with Braverman La Pove, 14, 22.

70. *Insurance Maps of San Francisco*, Vol. 8.

71. Jane Addams, *The Spirit of Youth and City Streets* (Urbana, Ill., New Edition, 1972), 78.

72. -------, *Twenty Years at Hull House* (New York, New Edition, 1962), 384.

73. *Emanu-El*, April 18, 1913, 14.

74. Interview with Braverman Lapove, 6, 24.

75. Dr. M.H. Harris, "Americanism and the Jew," *Jewish TImes and Observer*, January 19, 1912, 12.

76. *Emanu-El*, September 14, 1906, 3.

77. Hubert H. Brancroft, "San Francisco 1848-1850," *History of California*, 7 (San Francisco, 1888), 172; Frank Maryot, *Mountains and Molehills*, 167.

78. Frank Soule, John Gibson, James Nisbet, *The Annals of San Francisco* (New York, 1855), 258; Decker, *Fortunes and Failures*, 99-100.

79. K.M. Nesfeld, "The Jews from a Gentile Standpoint," *Overland Monthly*, 24 (April, 1895), 416-417; B.E. Lloyd, *Lights and Shades in San Francisco*, (San Francisco, 1876), 401.

80. Fears of overheated Americanization are discussed in *Emanu-El*, Jaunary 10, 1908, 2; Gus Ringolsky, "Immigration," *Jewish Times and Observer*, August 30, 1912, 4-6. On religious education see editorial by Rabbi Jacob Nieto in *Jewish Times and Observer*, January 5, 1912, 3; Interview with Dudune Solomon, 6. On aid to local synagogues see *Emanu-El*, October 4, 1907, 2.

81. *Emanu-El*, August 6, 1915, 16.

82. Herbert Gans, "Symbolic Ethnicity; The Future of Ethnic Groups and Cultures in America".

CHAPTER 4
AMBIVALENT HEROES;
ICONS OF SELF-IMAGE AMONG SAN FRANCISCO'S ITALIANS

The Bay Area's Italian cemetery lies in the city of Colma, a funeral town on the outskirts of San Francisco. A Duomo of sorts dominates the summit of the necropolis. It is the crypt of John Fugazi, a successful businessman and father-figure of the local colony. (Figure 15) Flanked by the Apostles Peter and Paul, the patron saints of Italian nationalism, a bust of the colony patriarch overlooks the resting place of his compatriots who, even at the moment of their death, chose symbolic repatriation.

All is not well in the cemetery. The proverbial tranquility of a man who has met his maker does not appear to envelop the Fugazi mausoleum. Agitated, gesturing saints and a scowling Fugazi grudgingly acknowledge that they do not preside over a hermetically sealed Italian colony. Further down the road, in the burial grounds of the Catholic church, once the arch-rival of Italian nationalism, the tombs of many prominent colonists contradict Fugazi's nostalgic concept of immigrant life. Other important colony figures have distanced themselves even further from Fugazi's designs by choosing non-denominational cemeteries.

These various patterns of funeral rites among San Francisco's Italians reflected a characteristically American ambivalence of culture, a paradoxical coupling of clashing sentiments and opposing impulses. On the one hand: the funeral monuments of colony leaders who shunned the local Italian cemetery yet saw no contradiction between their interment in organic American settings and their ethnic allegiances; On the other hand: the ethnic cemetery, devoted to preserving an old-world culture, but not entirely oblivious to the discovery of new horizons. Indeed, as the following pages suggest, a closer look at the funeral monuments surrounding John Fugazi's mausoleum reveals that American concepts of social and economic distinctions had infiltrated the seemingly hermetic Italian cemetery.

The cult heroes of local Italians also demonstrated this same ambivalence. Simultaneously, and with little sense of any inherent conflict, local Italians enshrined both Risorgimento hero Giuseppe Garibaldi as an emblem of strict ethnic loyalty, and an Americanized version of Christopher Columbus as a typically American pioneer.

The fusion of conflicting emotions among San Francisco's Italians reflected a peculiarly American cultural phenomenon. According to psychoanalyst Erik Erikson, "the functioning American, as the heir of a history of extreme contrasts and abrupt changes, bases his final ego identity on some tentative combination of dynamic polarities such as migratory and sedentary, individualistic and standardized, competitive and co-operative, pious and freethinking, responsible and cynical."[1] Perhaps nowhere were these abrupt changes and contrasts of turn-of-the-century America more apparent than in San Francisco, with its whirlwind development and quantum leap from boomtown to metropolis. Under such circumstances, newcomers from an Italy of equally sudden changes were ideally suited for the psychological state of existential ambivalence. Italians came to San Francisco actively seeking change; but the extreme rapidity of change occurring all around them meant, according to Herbert Gutman's analysis of culture in industrializing America, that they "lacked the time historically, culturally, and psychologically to be separated or alienated" from their cultural baggage.[2] San Francisco's Italians were, as Dino Cinel suggests, conservative adventurers, who embraced simultaneously the hierarchical social classifications of their indigenous background and the psychological, if not always realistic attractions of American egalitarian activities.[3]

During the initial stages of colony life, the American significance of the Italian outpost in San Francisco was mostly invisible to outsiders. Linguistically and symbolically the colony defined itself and its incertitudes in private Italian terms. Beginning in the early years of the twentieth century, Italian signs of ethnicity became much more visible to the rest of San Francisco; an Americanized and highly visible Columbus cult eclipsed the former popularity of the Italian Risorgimento hero Giuseppe Garibaldi. Sometime during the first decade of the twentieth century, the nature of colony festivals was altered as well. The celebration of Italian national holidays declined quite suddenly. Columbus Day, a holiday celebrated by all San Franciscans became, instead, the primary occasion for defining the contours of a new ethnic identity. Local Italians, began to pursue new and distinctly American ways of being Italian. They asserted their identity through the means of what Herbert Gans has called "symbolic ethnicity" : the identification with token aspects of indigenous ethnic worlds which could be manifested without having to disrupt American routines and mores.[4]

The origins of San Francisco's Italian colony have been recounted elsewhere and, for the purposes of this analysis of change and continuity in an American

108   Signs of Changes

city, a brief summary will suffice. Intense colony life had its origins in California's gold rush years. Approximately 260 Italians followed the gleam of gold to California in the 1850s. Many hoped to reap fortunes without actually digging for the precious metal. In San Francisco, where the real gold mines of commerce and trade flourished, twenty of the city's thirty-five Italians were traders, artisans, or professionals.[5] Between 1860 and 1880, improved trans-Atlantic travel and frequent economic crises lured growing numbers of Italians to the shores of the United States. Approximately 7,500 Italians chose California as their destination. By comparison, the states of New York and Louisiana—where the major debarkation ports from Italy were situated—had only a combined total of 8,500 documented Italian immigrants.[6]

An 1865 Italian consular report from San Francisco sheds light on the type of Italian who went to California. They were, the consul observed, compulsive gold hunters who arrived via Argentina, Peru, Chile, and Australia. When fabulous riches did not materialize in the El Dorados of their choice, these perpetual fortune seekers followed new rumors to the easily accessible San Francisco Bay. As seasoned veterans of previous gold rushes, California's Italians avoided involvement in economically fickle mining occupations. In the towns and cities of northern California, industrious Italian colonies "dedicat[ed] themselves to commerce and industries."[7] The census of 1870 supported the consul's observations. Approximately 18 percent of California's 5,000 Italians were engaged in trading professions. San Francisco's Italians showed an even higher disposition toward commerce. Over 38 percent earned their livelihood from peddling and trade. Few, if any, were unskilled manual laborers.[8] These veteran colonists hailed mostly from urban areas in northern Italy, the two largest groups being from Genoa, and the town of Lucca in the province of Tuscany.

The social composition of the colony changed significantly at the turn of the century with the growing influx of a new type of Italian immigrant to the United States. Economic stagnation provided the major impetus for Italian migration from the late nineteenth century and up till the First World War. Often, emigration offered the sole route of escape from a hopeless economic quagmire and explosive demographic pressures. The introduction of cheap ocean transportation and the lure of high wages furnished additional incentive. An insatiable demand for labor in the United States, bolstered by an immigration policy of benign neglect also played an important role in this immigration wave.[9]

Ron Robin

The new immigrants were, by and large, young males of rural descent. Most hailed from the South where illiteracy was the rule. Life in the New World was harsh and, consequently, economic expectations among newcomers were usually low: a brief sojourn in the United States accompanied by temporary relief from economic despair. Indeed, more than half of the Italian immigrants to the United States returned home after less than five years, and two out of every five returnees had been in America before.[10]

Italian migration to San Francisco generally followed the national picture. An Italian visitor in the city surmised that only half of the city's rapidly rising Italian population—about thirty thousand by 1910— had taken up permanent residence in San Francisco.[11] Despite its flamboyant history and its association with gold, San Francisco seemed to Italian sojourners to be just another urban center in a vast network of almost identical metropolises strewn throughout the United States. Although fortune seekers had once stalked its streets, "like wolves in search of prey," it was common knowledge among Italian immigrant laborers that San Francisco held out no better prospects than any other American city.[12]

The surge in Italian immigration to American cities induced rapid growth in San Francisco's colony, too. According to the Bureau of the Census, there were 5,212 people of Italian birth in San Francisco in 1890. This number ballooned to 7,508 in 1900, and 16,919 in 1910. In fact, more than thirty thousand San Franciscans— the foreign born and their children—claimed Italian as their native language in 1910.[13] As was the case in the rest of the country, the initial wave of newcomers brought an influx of southern Italians to San Francisco. By the mid-1880s, growing numbers of southerners, particularly from the provinces of Cosenza and Palermo, had infiltrated the previously northern colony. After 1907 however, northern Italians, the majority from the same regions as the original colonists, once again dominated the flow of newcomers. Yet in sharp contradiction to the background of old-time Italians in San Francisco, both southern and northern immigrants came from rural backgrounds. Even immigrants from the vicinity of the large cities of Genoa, Lucca, and Palermo hailed from farming communities on the outskirts of these urban centers.[14]

These mostly rural immigrants of the late nineteenth and early twentieth century encountered a well-established colony which had crystallized during or immediately following the Risorgimento, Italy's battle for national unification. Consequently, the internal world of the San Francisco colony reflected the political divisions and ethnic tensions of an Italy in its incipient years of

110 Signs of Changes

self-determination. The regional rivalries of a distant Italy as well as its political differences permeated the culture of the Italian colony in San Francisco. As the major issue of Italian politics of the early national period was the legitimacy of monarchial rule in Italy, the colony was divided sharply between Loyalists—a coalition of monarchists and conservatives who supported the government of the Royal House of Savoy—and those who espoused the Republican cause of the opposition. These political divisions often paralleled regional tensions, and the alignment between regional and political loyalties manifested itself quite openly in the local Italian newspapers.

A prominent publication in early colony life was *La Voce del Popolo*, founded by immigrants from Genoa in 1868. The tabloid was the self-proclaimed organ of the "National Party of California" which endorsed the Italian Republican cause. Italian domestic politics as well as local news from Genoa dominated its front page. Californian or American reports seldom found their way into *La Voce del Popolo*, and a daily column, "From The Capital," featured news from Rome, of course, and not from Washington. Along with *L'Italia*, which espoused the Loyalist cause and was supported by the Tuscan rivals of the local Genovese coalition, the colony's newspapers provided common grounds for communal life by re-creating images from the immigrants' homeland.

Explicitly Italian regional and political images were also the primary components of the colony's social life which evolved around local mutual aid societies. These voluntary organizations filled the vacuum of California's young and unformed state and local government by coordinating job opportunities, caring for the sick and needy, and burying the dead. In many ways mutual aid societies were like political parties, serving as rallying points in the colony's endless political struggles. Most Italian organizations in San Francisco were regional societies, such as the *Societa' di Mutua Soccorso dei Cavallegeri di Lucca*, established in 1874 for the benefit of immigrants from the vicinity of Lucca, in the province of Tuscany. Others, like the *Compagnia Garibaldina*, represented elites. Formed in 1868, the society was patronized by wealthy citizens who identified with Italy's legitimate government. A rival elite group, the *Compagnia Bersaglieri Italiani*, was an offshoot of an Italian radical Republican militia of the same name. Numerous societies were professional organizations. The *Societa' degli Agricoltori e Giardinieri*—the association of Italian produce gardeners founded in 1872—was probably the first such organization. Yet, the most important society transcended factionalism and regionalism. The *Societa'*

Ron Robin 111

di Mutua Beneficenza—founded in 1858—was open to all. By 1868 it had over a thousand members, approximately half of the Italian community. The *Societa'* founded the Italian cemetery and was contemplating the construction of a hospital for its members. Even though the society placed no restrictions on membership, transplanted Italian tensions based on regional origins and political alignments were quite evident in the internal struggles for leadership.[15]

Stoked by warring newspapers and fanned by the politics of mutual aid societies, the feuds of the homeland furnished fuel for what appeared to be peculiarly Italian disputes within the colony. Indeed, San Francisco's Italians persistently translated both American and international affairs into an Italian political lexicon, with little obvious relationship to their original context. In a society where everyone was either a Loyalist or Republican, even American concerns were presented in the symbolic language of Italian politics. Accordingly, the 1901 assassination of President William McKinley plunged the colony into a duel over the murder of Italy's King Umberto in 1900; he too, was the victim of an anarchist. The Loyalist *L'Italia* linked both assassinations to an international conspiracy, and accused the rival *La Voce del Popolo* of being an integral part of the international anarchist cause.[16] In the heat of the argument, McKinley was all but forgotten.

Because these internal skirmishes within the colony were carried out in the Italian language and relied on the idioms of a distant political context, most Americans were unable to decipher their meaning. Occasionally, when festering tensions within the colony erupted into street brawls, San Franciscans had a fleeting opportunity to glimpse the internal Italian world within their city. For the most part these internal skirmishes were hastily interpreted as evidence that the concerns of local Italians were far removed from the agenda of contemporary mainstream San Francisco. One such incident, of particularly violent dimensions erupted in 1894; it concerned the assassination of the President of France, Sadi Carnot, by an Italian anarchist. The debate in Italy focused on the degree to which the Italian government bore responsibility for the social torts and political conditions which had produced the murderer. Predictably, San Francisco's Italians, intensely involved in national causes, were drawn into the controversy.

A public meeting on the subject broke out into a brawl between loyalists and Republicans; it included a violent attack on the local Italian consul. As he emerged from the meeting hall, the startled consul found himself being chased through the streets of the Italian quarter by a "black mass of humanity ...

112   Signs of Changes

threatening, blaspheming, and denouncing." Miraculously he emerged unharmed, but internecine street brawls died down only after the police intervened.[17] According to the local English language press, the Sadi Carnot riots and similar street brawls of a political nature served as a metaphor for a vicarious post-Risorgimento struggle between Loyalists and their adversaries. An immutable concept of colony—the nurturing of an exclusive Italian identity and a concerted effort to persuade uprooted immigrants to focus on an ultimate return to their native land—appeared to be the only significant issues that preoccupied Italians in San Francisco.

Yet a structural examination of seemingly hermetic colonial symbols indicates otherwise. Subtle and sometimes not so subtle variations of Italian iconography in San Francisco suggest that though the language of culture was derived from an Italian context, its content exhibited many of those trends which one associates with the American setting, and, in particular, with the peculiarities of San Francisco's urban development. When a person attempts to articulate a novel concept, Ernst Gombrich observed in his study of the psychology of art, he or she invariably starts out with a familiar, previously learned "schema" followed by the superimposing of novel observations on the fundamental formula. Accordingly, San Francisco's Italians relied on the familiar idioms of their cultural baggage in coming to terms with their American surroundings, and articulated their changing concepts of culture on "the moving frontier" through modifications of familiar Italian *schema*.[18]

San Francisco's Italian cemetery, in particular its many monuments of personal concepts of culture furnishes a convenient point of departure for demonstrating the ambivalence of local Italians as expressed through the superimposing of American concepts on Italian schema. In its basic formula the Italian cemetery is a replica of a typical cemetery of Northern Italy. Like its nineteenth century Italian archetype, it has the layout of a city. Immaculate rows of vertical streets meet at centrally-placed piazzas. (Figure 16) In this city of the dead the orderly crossroads represent a meeting of minds, a shared sense of Italian identity among the inhabitants of this necropolis.[19]

The organization of space in the cemetery is characteristically hierarchical and centripetal. Like the typical Commune of northern Italy, the townplan of the necropolis enshrines social segregation. The cemetery's lowlands are occupied by the simple graves of ordinary colonists, which are occasionally interspersed with imposing edifices of stubborn aristocrats who chose to cling to old family plots

Ron Robin   113

rather than join their privileged peers in the more exclusive high grounds. Anchored along gently rising thoroughfares, and distinctly removed from the cluttered plots of the outlying areas, the smart mausoleums of the colony's elite lead uptown. There, at the summit, stands John Fugazi's Duomo-crypt. Time, Fugazi tomb suggests, is an inevitable, stately procession leading to a dramatic climax. In the case of his compatriots, that climax was an ultimate return to Italy, which even death could not deny.

These ethnocentric aspects notwithstanding, distinctly America concepts appear to have infiltrated the compulsive replication of indigenous Italian funeral rites. The overall organization of the cemetery and the architecture of the tombs depart significantly from their exclusive Italian context. A characteristically American version of social classification dictates the distinctions between elites and ordinary people in the cemetery. Distinguished family ties and tradition did not ensure an elite status in Colma. In fact, many colonists of notable origins, including veterans of the famed battles of the Risorgimento are buried in the lowlands. The elite section is composed of a plutocracy of dry-goods merchants, importers-exporters, and realtors who had achieved financial success due to the exceptional economic opportunities of the American city. The Fugazi family, for example, had risen to an eminent status in the colony due to their thriving maritime agency as well as their bank which attracted a large ethnic patronage.

The overall iconographic significance of the tombs in the elite section is culturally American, too, in its ambivalent fusing of ostentatious signs of hierarchical distinction, on the one hand, and egalitarian art forms on the other. The various elite crypts are private affairs, physically separate and closed off from the outside world with elaborate gates but, at the same time, they are architecturally and stylistically similar. This elaborate sameness, the counterpoising of repetitive patterns and complex ornamentation is, according to the criteria of anthropologists, typical of societies wavering between egalitarianism and social distinctions.[20] The architectural designs of egalitarian societies tend to be repetitive and, indeed, the art style of the mausoleums is repetitious; but the designs are elaborately repetitive as though indicating a simultaneous acceptance of hierarchy and equality of opportunity. This hovering between elitism and egalitarianism in architectural design, Henry Glassie suggests in his structural analysis of American architecture, is indicative of a culture "that is schizophrenically attracted at once—as American society is--to hierarchical social classification and to egalitarian activity."[21] In its broad social distinctions

114   Signs of Changes

as well as in its iconography, the Italian cemetery represents a typically American fusion of seemingly incompatible inclinations of indigenous ways and novel mores, a simultaneous acceptance of hierarchical classification and egalitarian philosophies.

Different priorities but an analogous mixture of metaphors are evident in the tomb of Andrea Sbarboro, Fugazi's main rival for the status of colony patriarch who was buried in the nearby Catholic Holy Cross cemetery. (Figure 17) To begin with, a radically different concept of space permeates the design of the ground upon which Sbarboro's mausoleum is implanted. Holy Cross is not a pedantic town of the dead. In an elaborate homage to American individualism, graves are strewn throughout the lawned grounds without a conspicuous plan in mind. There are few paths and no boulevards upon the rolling hills. Burial spots seem to have been chosen on a whim. The plots do not appear to be divided up according to any obvious criteria, such as national origin. The monuments of Irish descendants rest alongside those of Italian co-religionists. Subtle distinctions do exist of course in Holy Cross. Sbarboro is buried in what might be called the financial district; his nearby neighbor is Amadeo Gianinni, the founder of the Bank of America.

Tombstones are distinguishable more by personal taste than ethnic tradition. A distinctly American fondness for individualism is articulated through the seemingly unplanned placement of tombstones, and the private style of each individual plot. Sbarboro who, among other things was a prominent savings and loan banker, is entombed in an appropriate bank-like sepulcher. In this wonderful blend of piety and pragmatism, Sbarboro's own individual calling as a banker is given precedence over any other social allegiance, ethnic or religious. On a purely internal colonial level, Sbarboro's tomb presents a striking fusion of antonyms. One can be a loyal colonist, the tomb suggests, without rejecting the Catholic Church, formerly the mortal enemy of Italian nationalism. An additional fusion of differences is exhibited within the mausoleum itself where a mural of an angel hovering over a rural landscape—perhaps Italian, perhaps Californian— espouses Sbarboro's call to local Italians to create a cultural oxymoron: "an Italy in California."[22]

This blending of opposites was not reserved for funeral rites. A similar coupling of seemingly incompatible guidelines appears to have dictated the Italian colony's choice of cult heroes, in particular the simultaneous celebration of Giuseppe Garibaldi and Christopher Columbus. Giuseppe Garibaldi, the leader and catalyst of Italy's armed struggle for unification, had traditionally furnished an attractive rallying point for the city's entire colony, Republicans and Loyalists. Garibaldi's dedication to freedom and self-determination on two continents—he led campaigns of national liberation in his own country as well as in Brazil and Uruguay—endowed him with an international aura that appealed to Italians in exile. Garibaldi was also above mundane political squabbling. Although a Republican at heart, the Italian freedom fighter was willing to accept national independence in Italy under any institutional form, including monarchy. To a certain degree, Garibaldi personified the ideal to which all Italian sojourners were expected to adhere. He, too, had found temporary shelter in the United States, but indelible ties eventually led him back to Italy. All Italians, irrespective of political allegiances, cherished his memory.

Garibaldi's counterpoise in the Italian colonial mind in San Francisco was Christopher Columbus, the proverbial discoverer of the American continent who, in many ways, reflected the ambivalent sentiments of San Francisco's transplanted Italians. Columbus was a pragmatic immigrant who had immersed himself personally, politically, and culturally into the world of a foreign state without too many regrets. In contrast to the Garibaldi theme his allegiance to an Italian context was a token one at best. With growing intensification he was presented as an Italian version of the classic American adventurer who had followed the call of a peculiarly American Manifest Destiny.

The co-existence between these two contradictory cult heroes was, however, not static. Even though local Italians persistently sought guidance from both folk figures, their iconographic significance underwent frequent changes. Both in plastic form and in folk festivals a significant shift in the balance between Garibaldi and Columbus reflected a reorientation of Italian self-image within an American city. Over the years, the ceremonial depictions of the two cult heroes signalled a shift both in communal identity and in perceptions of the city. The changing of the guard among colony cult heroes also reflected a more general process by which San Francisco's "privatism" of early stages of urbanization was replaced by the realities of urban-industrial interdependence.

The Garibaldi cult had arrived in San Francisco when it was still dominated by a boom town mentality. The image of the Risorgimento hero served as protector against the general confusion of dislocating surroundings. His own orderly experiences provided a paradigm for Italians in San Francisco. Italian immigrants had left a turbulent homeland and moved to an equally fluid environment. Under these confusing circumstances, local Italians defined their lives according to traditional models which allowed them to interpret their novel surroundings within the framework of comprehensible patterns. Garibaldi, an exemplary hero rooted firmly in an almost mythological period, provided San Francisco's Italians with a sense of stability. Yet, at the same time, the artistic forms used to depict the General departed significantly from the Italian tradition.

The iconography of Garibaldi in San Francisco was removed from his original political context. In Italy, his life had been depicted with the fervor of a passion play. The Garibaldi cult in Italy involved epic portrayals of the General departing with his troops to conquer Sicily, his Christ-like sufferings at the battle of Aspremonte, and compassionate portrayals of the crestfallen hero in self-imposed exile on the island of Capra after failure to unite the Italian peninsula into one political entity.

Two common denominators permeated the traditional hagiography of Garibaldi in his homeland. Most often he appeared as a dynamic, active fellow. The generic Garibaldi picture was not that of a venerable hero posing sedately for a portrait. Instead, he was actively engaged in fighting foes, exhorting compatriots, or mourning his defeats. An additional element which invariably appeared in these pictures was a rich and meaningful background. Garibaldi was usually surrounded by his troops or placed within a detailed depiction of those landscapes in which he had either triumphed or failed.[23]

By contrast, the image of Garibaldi in San Francisco was superimposed on a distinctly different background and with a very different sense of movement in mind. The Italian newspapers in the city produced curt, motionless portraits, usually against a white, featureless background. Representations of Garibaldi interacting with other people or performing a historical feat were rare. For the most part he appeared in cropped bust portraits, as in the illustration in the July 4, 1907 commemorative edition of *L'Italia*. (Figure 18)

The most obvious element of these curt visual descriptions superimposed upon a neutral background was the removal of this exemplary hero from a well-known sequence of historic events. Garibaldi in the crowded hagiographic depictions of his homeland had occupied a particular location in time and space. The epigrammatic San Francisco Garibaldi, on the other hand, was removed from any actual setting; he represented, instead, an abstract symbol. This symbolic Garibaldi was spatially and temporally free to experiment with novel surroundings. The San Francisco depictions of Garibaldi represented a

Ron Robin 117

self-conception which was much in tune with local surroundings. The emphasis here was on coming to terms with a new and still incoherent cultural setting, rather than a paradigmatic repetition of an exiled hero's deeds. The curt depiction of a familiar figure reflected the private experiences of Italians in San Francisco; his exemplary character, rather than his role in a particular historic sequence of events, was the primary component of his portrayals in San Francisco.

Garibaldi placed within Risorgimento circumstances was an artifact of a real Italian past; a cropped Garibaldi and an attendant featureless background was a by-product of an indefinite American present. In this sense, Garibaldi's 1907 depiction in the centennial edition of the loyalist *L'Italia* signalled a change in fortunes for this cult hero. The linking of the Risorgimento hero with other cultural and temporal circumstances represented a turning point in his iconographic appearances. It appeared that, by 1907, even the intransigent editors of *L'Italia* who favored an introspective colony experience, were willing to acknowledge the shift in social perspectives. No more did they posit their own particularistic experience as the exclusive or dominant centerpiece. Garibaldi's sharing of the limelight with George Washington acknowledged a growing awareness that the walls of the colony were far from impenetrable. The juxtaposition of an introspective colony symbol with a culturally external figure recognized the complex, intertwining nature of American surroundings.

Traditionally, Garibaldi's birthday, which fell on July Fourth, had allowed colony irredentists of the mostly Loyalist faction to define cultural distinctions between themselves and mainstream society. While San Francisco celebrated American independence day, Italian colonists could mark their own introspective national experience. Not surprisingly, on July 4, 1907, the centennial of Garibaldi's birth, an entire edition of the Loyalist *L'Italia* recounted his life struggles. The national holiday of the United States was summarily dismissed with faint praise. Buried between the many articles on Garibaldi, the newspaper noted in passing that it was merely a "happy coincidence that both these great occasions fall on the same day."[24]

Yet the newspaper's deliberate Italian bias on July 4, 1907 was belied by the banner illustration on the front page. The large sketch of the "two lions"—Giuseppe Garibaldi and George Washington—was quite ambivalent. (Figure 18) Of equal size, Garibaldi and Washington shared the spotlight. In contrast to the dominant tone of Italian nationalism in the written message, the newspaper did not give visual precedence to the Italian motif. Instead, the illustration juggled the seemingly incompatible symbols of an ethnocentric Italian heritage and a distinctly local American context. Although they had never met due to the "span of time that intervened between their lives," the newspaper had no doubt that together they would have accomplished great missions.[25]

Despite this attempt to fuse past with present, the iconographic alignment of the two lions signaled that the conjecturing of a kindred spirit between Washington and Garibaldi as respective symbols of Italian nationalism and an American way of life, was somewhat contrived. Both heroes were boxed into isolated frameworks which not even the spanning wings of the Eagle of Courage could pierce. According to the accompanying article, "Garibaldi and America," the problem was that the Italian hero's life had no bearing on American events. Had he accepted a post in the Union army during the Civil War, the newspaper speculated, then he would have been a much more usable symbol.[26]

The removal of Garibaldi from the centerpiece, and his alignment with another hero from a different setting was a benchmark in the gradual recognition of Garibaldi's irrelevance as symbol of a local San Francisco experience. To be sure, as late as 1910, the irredentist *L'Italia* still lectured its readers that the commemoration of a foreign day of independence was inappropriate. For those who felt the urge to celebrate, *L'Italia* admonished, "we should remember that on this same day of the Fourth of July, Giuseppe Garibaldi was born."[27] By 1913, extravagant celebrations of Garibaldi's birthday had all but ceased. In fact, the life and times of the Risorgimento hero no longer dominated the news in *L'Italia* on the day of his birth. In 1913, and in an abrupt departure from its former policy, the loyalist newspaper joined its English-language counterparts in declaring the Fourth of July an official holiday for its employees. Editorials no longer referred to independence day as the celebration of other people. In fact, the appointment of an Italian grand marshall for the city's Fourth of July Parade of 1913 warranted greater attention than the now hazy accounts of Giuseppe Garibaldi's battles.[28]

The waning of the Garibaldi cult did not leave local Italians without an exemplary cult hero. Christopher Columbus, a hitherto minor hero, took over from Garibaldi as colony center piece. Heightened identification with the discoverer of the American continent accompanied colony disengagement from the life and times of Garibaldi. The symbolism inherent in the escapades of an itinerant sailor appeared to eclipse the fast-fading apparitions of a remote fatherland. San Francisco's Italians had celebrated Columbus day as early as

Ron Robin 119

1869. But with the fading of Garibaldi's attractiveness, the celebration of the sailor from Genoa soared. The pomp surrounding Chicago's World's Columbian exhibition of 1893 enhanced Columbus's symbolic stature too. His triumph in mainstream American circles most certainly alerted local Italians to their countryman's potential as a wonderfully ambivalent symbol, suspended somewhere between an old and new home. Indeed, transcending his Italian context, Columbus fit into the mold of the classic American adventurer who, like the Forty-niner and other American pioneers, had followed the call of Manifest Destiny in contributing towards a future American empire.[29]

Declared an official California State holiday in 1909, Columbus Day became a major focal point through which San Francisco's Italians asserted their identity. Before huge crowds of San Franciscans of all ethnic backgrounds, and with the co-sponsorship of numerous non-Italian communal organizations, the Italian colony ritually re-enacted the story of Columbus's landing in the new world. The annual pageantry allowed local Italians to assert the relevance of their own culture in a distinctly American setting.[30] In 1909, two years after Garibaldi's centennial swan song, even the loyalist *L'Italia* adopted the new symbol by enticing new suscribers with a poster of Columbus "in fourteen colors" and accompanied by "thirty or so other persons."[31] This picture—L'Italia never revealed its source to its readers—ultimately became the newspaper's symbol. (Figure 19) Well into the late 1920s, the picture was reprinted in all of L'Italia's commemorative editions, not only on Columbus Day.[32]

In contrast to the actionless and lifeless portraits of Garibaldi, Columbus, in this and in other depictions, was surrounded by many people and appeared to be actively performing a historical deed of much relevance to local Italians. Columbus the discoverer represented a "new Homo Americanus, more easily identified by his mobility than by his habitat."[33] The cult of Garibaldi had suggested, at least subtly, that the Italian experience in San Francisco was meaningful only insofar as it reproduced at least a modified version of Garibaldi's experience of exile and return. The Columbus depicted in *L'Italia* departed from this philosophy. Despite the paraphernalia of cultural baggage represented by the flags of a distant empire, Columbus and his peers were obviously moving away from the European point of departure, and towards a Terra Incognita. Rather than merely sanctifying the sailor-discoverer, the picture posited him among a motley group of mobile peers, some piously kneeling, others gazing with a mixture of curiosity and contempt at a pristine location where nothing appeared

120   Signs of Changes

to be pre-empted by history or tradition. Neither indigenous inhabitants nor significant natural phenomena intruded upon the act of taking possession of new circumstances. As for the landscape of discovery, it was no more than a generic beach. In an age of firm belief in the doctrine of geographical determinism, this piece of ordinary landscape could be could made over to suit a variety of fantasies concerning the essence of American life.

The cultural significance of these iconographical transitions from the introspectiveness of the Garibaldi cult to the ambivalently American setting of Columbus may be verified by examining shifts in other aspects of colony life. The political tone of colony newspapers changed along with its heroes. By the turn of the century, the Republican *La Voce del Popolo* had altered its motto from "Organ of the Italian National Party" to the more neutral "Organ of the Italian Population in California." The newspaper also revised its format. News reports from Italy still lingered on, but the front page now featured local San Francisco items. By 1911, the Loyalist *L'Italia* succumbed to changing times by dropping its motto of "Life and Struggle in Defense of the Italian Cause." Instead, the tabloid adopted an insipid "Echo of Italian Colonies and their Interests on the Pacific Coast." The shifts in slogans corresponded to the shift in colony heroes from inner-directed Italian experiences to those of shared arrangements with other Americans.

Along these same lines, San Francisco's Italians also modified their formerly ostentatious celebrations of September 20, the anniversary of Italian national sovereignty in Rome. As a significant opportunity to express their cultural self-perception, the changing content and intensity of September 20 celebrations heralded the mutation of concepts of colony as well as perceptions of American surroundings. The turning-point in September 20 celebrations appears to have occurred in 1895, a year after the infamous Sadi Carnot street brawls, and the thirtieth anniversary of Italian national sovereignty in Rome. As was the case every year before this Italian equivalent of the Fourth of July, local Republicans had launched their traditional fall offensive against Loyalist counterparts. This particular year, disagreement was ostensibly sparked by contention over who should have the honor of organizing the anniversary celebrations. Local Republicans claimed that the attack on Rome had been led by their Bersalgieri mentors, and therefore they should lead the anniversary celebrations. Loyalists countered-attacked with their claims for prerogative as representatives of the legitimate Italian monarchy. Tempers flared further when local Republicans

Ron Robin 121

objected to the fact that the predominately Loyalist San Francisco delegation to the September 20 in Rome had had a private audience with the Italian monarch.[34]

Yet, what appeared to be a transplantation of Italian differences to a colonial setting was, in actual fact, an elaborate scenery for a distinctly local dispute over patronage within an American context. The seemingly intransigent battle lines between Republicans and Loyalists dissipated almost over night. A pragmatic compromise regarding the mode of celebrating Italian independence suggests that local civic issues, rather than entrenched Italian differences were behind the ritual re-enactment of Risorgimento politics in San Francisco. Republicans abruptly awarded their rivals the exclusive rights to organize the September 20 celebration in Washington Square—the heart of the predominantly Italian North Beach district—after being promised that they would receive all surplus festivity funds to distribute among the colony's poor and needy.[35] Both sides abandoned seemingly unyielding stands when confronted with an opportunity for enhancing their patronage, and bolstering the ranks of their troops. These troops were needed for extra-colonial functions, in particular the supplying of Italian votes for local municipal and state political elections. America's political machine's had discovered the Italian vote and hoped to use the colonial structure of cohesive mutual aid societies as sources for ballot stuffing.[36]

Ultimately, the compromise of 1895 failed miserably. The Loyalist organizers had spent lavishly, and no surplus funds remained. In fact a huge and somewhat suspicious deficit which emerged from the celebration hastened the collapse of the precarious ceasefire between Loyalists and their adversaries. Republicans had failed to gain patronage through a charity drive, while the squandering of funds explicitly earmarked for an Italian celebration raised questions as to whether a national Italian event was, indeed, the appropriate tool for mustering troops for local issues.[37]

Indeed, after the 1895 celebrations, conspicuous commemoration of September 20 declined rapidly. By 1909, the colony ignored the event completely. In following years the anniversary of Italian sovereignty in Rome was celebrated modestly and sporadically, with gala evenings reserved for the colony's elite and the occasional picnic organized by the local Dante Alighieri Society.[38] Italian colonies in the isolated provincial cities of California continuously marked the occasion with pomp. San Francisco's Italians, faced with a variety of ways of

122   Signs of Changes

expressing their changing concept of culture in a cosmopolitan American metropolis chose, by contrast, to avoid exclusive expression of their aspirations through the idiom of Italian nationalism.[39]

The decline of the local Garibaldi cult, the discarding of nationalistic slogans by local newspapers, and the demise of intensely Italian celebrations, were all the result of a crisis in the conventional apparatus of colonial structure. A growing awareness of the intrusions of foreign bodies into the colony, and of the interconnecting aspects of urban life which linked Italians with a wide range of complex issues, demanded a reorientation of culture.

The need to foster a new sense of identity for local Italians was apparent as early as 1897, when a local colony leader observed with alarm a marked drop in enrollment in mutual aid societies. Newcomers, Carlo Dondero observed, were apparently oblivious to the re-creation of Italian issues in the new world. By the early twentieth century, the isolated structure of Italian life in San Francisco was ruptured as the city was integrated into the nation-wide, economic and cultural metropolitan network. The desire to have things both ways—to accept the fruits of American abundance without abandoning the fundamentals of an old order—had once been reserved for the colony's economic elite, the brokers between the colony and American society. Now, the growing pressures of extra-colonial bodies seeking Italian support also allowed ordinary colonists to partake in the American experience of existential ambivalence.

The decline of mutual aid societies and the rise of involvement in mainstream issues among San Francisco's Italians was not caused by a single factor. The veteran colonial elite attributed the demise of national identity to the new type of Italian immigrant who was poor, of rural descent, and quite oblivious to the political squabblings of the urban bourgeoisie.[40] Indeed, a significant gap separated veteran colonists from newcomers. Most veteran colonists hailed from Italy's politically conscious northern cities, and nurtured their self-awareness in a nationalistic environment. Their subsequent removal from Italy and their unfamiliarity with the social trends among rural immigrants encouraged them to couch their experiences in the only language with which they were quite familiar, that of the Risorgimento.

By contrast, the new immigrants of the late nineteenth and early twentieth century were largely unaffected by the Italian nationalist movement. For the most part, the Italian national spirit passed over rural Italy. Insensitivity among Italy's exclusively urban, middle-class politicos to the plight of rural areas, continuing economic despair in the agricultural sector, and chronic social fragmentation limited peasant interests to local surroundings in which the bell of the local parish church could be heard. This phenomenon of Campanalismo, the indifference of rural Italians to national issues, challenged the frozen Risorgimento apparatus of colony cultural structure in San Francisco.[41]

Italian peasant newcomers were much more interested in achieving the often elusive dream of owning land rather than re-enacting the national wars of Italy. San Francisco's vast agricultural hinterlands drove home a realization that land ownership was more feasible in "Italy in California" than back home.[42] The city was the hub of a fertile and sparsely settled state. The lure of unsettled territories and the possibility of land ownership sparked strong emotions among many of San Francisco's peasant newcomers. California, a folk song from Tuscany suggested, offered tired and disillusioned peasants the opportunity to own land and spend "beautiful evenings; neither troubled by thoughts nor melancholy feelings."[43] "Why should I return" to Italy, mused an Italian immigrant peasant in California, "if I am doing so well here?"[44]

Even more destructive to group solidarity than the lure of land ownership was the impact of American labor unions upon colony life. Organized labor provided an alternative framework for the development of relevant cultural benchmarks. Although the American east coast experience did not augur favorably for the relationship between Italians and labor unions, anti-Italian sentiment in the Bay Area was less apparent because the local status of Italians differed from the norm. In addition to sheltered job opportunities furnished by Italian-owned enterprises in the Bay Area, newcomers specialized in fields, such as fishing and produce gardening, which did not threaten the city's union labor force. Moreover, local Italians enjoyed the unusual honor of being categorized as "white" workers. San Francisco's large Chinese and Japanese communities shouldered the blame for undermining blue collar wages—an accusation often levelled against Italians in other American cities.[45] Widespread demand for their skills added to the prestige of Italian workers. Non-Italian produce farmers actively sought the hiring of skilled Italian agriculturists, and local food processing firms, many of them Italian owned, offered over 600 seasonal posts for Italian women during the summer months.[46]

Despite these favorable circumstances, Italian newcomers had no ties with organized labor during the nineteenth century, because the predominantly craft-oriented unions ignored white unskilled laborers. In 1891, the Building

124 Signs of Changes

Trades Council—the Enfant Terrible of San Francisco's unions—even inserted an anti-immigrant plank into its legislative platform. Some Italians observers mistakenly interpreted the action of the builders' union as a general sign of discord between all unions and Italians in San Francisco.[47] Nonetheless, relations developed favorably. By the turn of the century, union labor throughout the United States sought additional political maneuverability by organizing unskilled laborers. Within this context, professional organizers of the American Federation of Labor (A.F.L.) were sent to San Francisco. Among the city's many immigrant groups, Italians received special attention.[48]

The A.F.L. was probably attracted by Italian laborers' near-monopoly of various economic activities, from produce gardening to garbage disposal. Workers in these sectors often belonged to professional guilds for the protection of their members and the enhancement of the political careers of affluent benefactors. In furthering their interests these societies readily offered their votes to accommodating politicians.[49] Workingmen societies such as the Scavengers' Union, the Produce Gardeners Association, and the Italian Fishermen's Association were not organized around class. They were the creation of colony potentates who hoped to use them as political weapons within the confines of the colony. Allegiances were usually professional or regional. Ties with organized labor were non-existent until the early twentieth century when, as part of a nation-wide campaign to enlist unskilled laborers, local union leaders sought access to this potential reservoir of support for their cause.

One of the A.F.L.'s first campaigns to organize unskilled laborers in the Golden State at the turn of the century was among Italian laborers in Southern California. Success prompted union officials to attempt a similar campaign in San Francisco. Efforts focused on attracting Italians by issuing promotional material in Italian, particularly among streetcar construction workers in the aftermath of the earthquake and fire of 1906. Over 1,200 of these laborers joined the ranks of organized labor; many, according to the organizers, were Italians.[50] By 1903, Union Local 8944, the major body of organized unskilled workers in San Francisco, had a large, active Italian contingent.[51]

Organized labor introduced a large segment of the Italian colony into mainstream San Francisco society by offering social frames of reference that transcended a stagnant concept of ethnicity. These windows into American society, coupled with the immigrants' lack of interest with Italian politics, challenged the viability of established colony frameworks. Much to the detriment

Ron Robin 125

of San Francisco's veteran Risorgimento colonists, Italians newcomers used their culture as a device for improving their personal, distinctly non-nationalistic lot in life.

An additional blow to the hitherto closed colony life came from the Catholic church, one of the main acculturizing bodies for Italian newcomers throughout the United States. Cordial ties between the Catholic Church and Italian immigrants were by no means inevitable. The Church had earned the animosity of nationalistic Italians—the bulk of colony veterans—for its opposition to the political unification of Italy. Peasants, too, expressed little love for the Church. The Catholic establishment in Italy had tacitly supported the efforts of local potentates in keeping the poor powerless. A distant, anti-national, elitist Church encouraged widespread anti-clericalism among all Italians.[52]

In the United States, relations between Church and Italian newcomers appeared to be heading toward an even worse state of affairs, as the American Church attempted to eradicate local customs which had preserved Italian links with religion. Despite their animosity towards the Church, Italy's working classes had maintained their faith in Catholicism because local religious practices provided a reassuring, tangible presence in a harsh world. Time-honored folk customs were integrated into local liturgy, and pagan gods were purified by assuming the garb of local saints.[53] The American Church, dominated by Irish prelates, objected to the injection of folk ways into Catholic liturgy, in particular the colorful worship of local patron saints. The ecclesiastic hierarchy feared a rekindling of nativist questioning of the Church's patriotism and its religious practices which menaced the refined values of the Republic. Clashes between Irish and Italian newcomers over jobs and housing further complicated the uneasy rapport between an Irish-dominated Church and the Italian immigrant.[54]

In San Francisco, too, the Catholic Church favored its Irish parishioners. The *Monitor*, the official organ of the Catholic Archdiocese of San Francisco, initially defined itself as "an Irish-Catholic newspaper."[55] Even after the turn of the century, the news and views expressed in this weekly publication were still aimed at a predominantly Gaelic constituency. The *Monitor's* motto, "For Faith and Fatherland," concisely expressed the Church's goals in San Francisco: the establishment of a modus vivendi between an all-embracing Catholicism and American nationalism. This policy received little sympathy from the veteran Italian colony. As late as 1904, the *Monitor* still recalled the hissing at passing priests and the actions of "members of the Garibaldi guards and the Bersaglieri

126　　　　　　　　　　　　　　　　　　　　　　　　　　　Signs of Changes

[who] used to persuade the more simple immigrants that the unification of Italy made it impossible for a man to be a Catholic and a loyal Italian at the same time."[56] As in the East, newcomers' processions of saints met with opposition from the Irish clergy who felt uncomfortable with these manifestations of "pagan Mediterraneans."[57]

These tensions notwithstanding, the Catholic Church in San Francisco appeared more attuned than its east coast counterparts to the needs of ethnic groups. In the Bay Area, where the influx of immigrants had always been a source of strength for Catholicism, national churches had existed since the 1870s; the French church of "Notre Dame des Victoires" went back as far as 1856. On the east coast, national parishes were established only in the 1890s.[58] As far as local Italians were concerned, the Church discreetly, but actively, reacted to the changing currents within the colony. As a token of its earnest attempts at rapprochement, the official Catholic press in San Francisco judiciously avoided any condemnation of local September 20 celebrations commemorating the fall of Papal Rome.[59] Yet, compared to the favorable attitude of the Archdiocese to most ethnic Catholics in San Francisco, the initial gestures of the Catholic establishment toward its proverbial stepchildren were modest.

At first, the small number of Italians seeking sacrament held services in the basements of other parish churches. Eventually, in 1884, the Italian parish of SS. Peter and Paul was established.[60] The last ethnic church to be built in nineteenth-century San Francisco, its obscure location on the corner of Dupont—later named Grant—and Filbert streets conveyed uncertainty over its future. Most Italians resided in an area north of Broadway and west of Telegraph Hill. Yet the Italian church was erected on the extreme north-east periphery of the colony, on the slopes of Telegraph Hill. While land constraints may have been behind its remote location, pictures from the 1880s indicate the availability of more centrally-placed sites.[61] In addition to its remote location, the church's general appearance confirmed that SS. Peter and Paul had been constructed with much trepidation concerning its future. The Catholic hierarchy in San Francisco considered ethnic churches to be "temporary by their very nature" and as such sought to lower costs of their construction by using cheap and disposable wood.[62] Yet a glance at the various national churches raises the suspicion that some ethnic parishes were considered more temporary than others. The German churches of St. Anthony and St. Boniface were built of stone, as was the French church of Notre Dame des Victoires.[63] That of SS. Peter and Paul was made of wood, possibly the most simple and least ornate structures in the Archdiocese. (Figure 20) The edifice was also markedly smaller than other churches in the area. Squeezed in between residential structures, SS. Peter and Paul occupied a small portion of its 19,000 square feet lot. In comparison, the nearby Episcopal church of St. Paul dominated its 5,260 square feet site, and the Catholic church of St. Francis engulfed most of its 15,000 square feet lot.[64]

One of the Church's first signs of growing confidence in San Francisco's Italians took place in 1896, at the height of turmoil and confusion over Italian nationalism in the colony. In the aftermath of Italy's costly colonial campaigns in Ethiopia, services were held in San Francisco's Italian church for the soldiers who had fallen in the Italian state's first large-scale national escapade. The memorial ceremony indicated the Catholic Church's willingness to appease its Italian parishioners, for near the altar in SS. Peter and Paul stood a catafalque adorned with an Italian national flag.[65] A conciliatory gesture of this nature—the presence of the emblem of a secular Italy in the heart of a Catholic sanctuary—would have been difficult to imagine in Italy.

In 1897, an additional indication of reconciliation and faith in the future was heralded by the arrival of the Italian-based Salesian brothers, an order specializing in serving immigrant Italians. The Salesian brothers were Transigenti, Catholic priests who accepted Italian nationalism as a Fait Accompli.[66] The Salesians also allowed the injection of personal saints in their liturgy, thereby replenishing ties between Church and peasant newcomers. Ironically, by the early twentieth century, it was the veteran colonists, and not the Church who objected to the processions of saints.[67] The Italian priests' acknowledgment of nationalist sentiment and an understanding of the immigrant peasant culture had healed many festering wounds from the days of their dogmatic Jesuit predecessors. Growing numbers of Italians joined the Catholic Church under the Salesians. By 1898, the Order even consecrated an additional church for Italian produce gardeners residing in the present-day suburb of Ocean View.[68]

The Italian parish at the turn of the century provided a sense of direction for a culture in a state of flux. As representatives of the singular and most powerful institution in this predominantly Catholic city, the Salesian brothers opened channels for increased participation of newcomers in the affairs of the surrounding American society. In addition, San Francisco's Catholic Church also allowed old-time colonists to maintain their concept of ethnic awareness through the tacit acceptance of Italian nationalism. In fact, a national parish offered a

128 Signs of Changes

dignified alternative to street brawls and the intricacies of Risorgimento politics. The presence of a sympathetic Italian priesthood reiterated the Catholic Church's recognition of transitions in the points of reference for identity within the colony. Church and colony cooperation in the swift construction of a temporary abode for SS. Peter and Paul after the earthquake of 1906, followed by plans for an auspicious permanent structure, constituted the most tangible sign of changing times.

In the aftermath of the destruction by earthquake and fire, initial designs for a permanent Italian parish were imposing but somewhat out of tune with colony desires. Plans called for a solemn, baroque-style building which resembled many other churches in the Bay Area yet lacked any sense of Italian relevance.[69] These intentions were never implemented. The reconstruction of an ethnic house of worship furnished a golden opportunity to create a monument of self-expression, and the colony's leading financial and commercial enterprises contributed enthusiastically and generously towards a more explicit architectural display of ethnic identity. In 1924, the new, permanent, and ambivalently Italo-American church of SS. Peter and Paul was consecrated.

A pair of surging Neo-gothic towers dominated the 1924 Romanesque structure which meant to inspire "a renewed feeling of a little of Italy" and perhaps a little something else.[70] Apparently, a reliance on the internal harmony of the Romanesque did not express the necessary compatibility with exuberant surroundings. Skyscraping towers filled this vacuum with a brazen magnitude so dear to urbanites in America. (Figure 21) The Neo-gothic turrets infused the sentimental Romanesque church with typically American aspirations. An explicit message of reconciliation between Italians and the Church was to be displayed in an unusual mosaic over the main facade. With traditional scenes from the holy scriptures came a depiction of two lay figures: Christopher Columbus disembarking on American soil, and Dante Alighieri "writing the first verse of the Paradise" from his Divine Comedy. Both figures represented the two "highest glories of medieval Italy."[71] The choice of the High Middle Ages formulated an appropriate compromise between the aspirations of the Church, the competing concepts of Italian ethnic pride within the colony, and the special qualities of American city life. The High Middle Ages were the golden age of Italian culture; a generation of Italian cultural giants stalked the earth. Yet, much to the advantage of the Church, the creation of a modern Pan-Italian cultural entity did not induce political unity in the peninsula. The geographical expanse known as

Italy remained fragmented. Nationalism was still in a state of infancy. Only the universal Catholic Church transcended the confines of petty despots.

The inclusion of lay figures on the facade of a modern Catholic church was unorthodox, if not unprecedented. It expressed the Church's eagerness to lead the city's stray sheep back into the fold. For those still sustaining some remnants of their cultural heritage, the mosaics also furnished a degree of national pride. Dante and Columbus also constituted an excellent foundation upon which to build a spiritual link between Italy and the immigrant's newly-found home. Both Dante and Columbus had demonstrated the importance of flexibility in their adaptation to changing circumstances. Their acceptance of change appealed to American city people, always on the verge of moving on to new horizons. Columbus was the epitome of the wandering Italian, forced to seek his fortune on foreign soil yet proud of his origin. He represented the physical link between one people and two distant lands. Dante provided the cultural link. The great poet had advocated the use of a common tongue based on the dialect of his native Tuscany. His new, almost artificial language furnished the first modern common denominator for the inhabitants of the Italian peninsula. Like San Francisco's Italians, Dante had used his cultural background to create a synthetic tool of adaptation which was appropriate for the political and social context of a new society.

The Catholic Church, like the labor unions, provided alternative frames of reference for Italian immigrants in San Francisco, particularly for the recent arrivals of peasant descent. Yet, in addition to the outside influences on Italian culture in the city, the contours of colony life were also eroding internally. The changing cultural morphology of San Francisco's Italian colony in the early twentieth century was not attributable only to indifferent newcomers and the strength of competing social frameworks outside of the colony. By the turn of the century, internal factional warfare among veteran colonists was inextricably entangled with their extra-colonial business interests. The colony's elite had reaped substantial profits from their protracted stay in the Bay Area as well as from the continuous influx of newcomers. By the early twentieth century, few could close their eyes to the fact that partisanship had become less important than its lucrative side effects.

On the one hand stood those who gained from a continuous acceptance of traditional concepts of "colony," an allegiance to the Italian body politic, and a moral commitment to return to Italy. Travel agents and immigrant bankers led

130 Signs of Changes

this faction. Their acknowledged leader was the Loyalist Fugazi, the local representative of Banco Di Napoli, the Italian government's official channel for funneling immigrant money back to Italy. The prosperity of his travel agency and banking ventures hinged upon a continuous flow of Italians to and from their homeland. On the other side of the barrier stood those who profited from an indefinite sojourn of local Italians. Investment bankers and real estate brokers, such as Andrea Sbarboro and Amadeo Giannini of Bank of America fame, treated the eventual return to Italy in the abstract. They urged immigrants to fulfill their desires for land and property ownership in California. As real estate agents and founders of building societies they stood to gain political power in California politics while reaping immense profits from a stable Italian presence in the Golden State.[72]

The entanglement of political patronage and business interests widened the gap between colonists and the original spirit of Italian nationalism. By 1910, the old divisions of Loyalists and Republicans seemed to have lost their vigor. New battle lines were formed between pragmatists, those who saw the fate of immigrants inextricably tied to the California soil, and irredentists, who demanded at least token allegiance to the idea of an eventual return to Italy. The longevity of both factions hinged upon their maintaining a preferred status among Italians in San Francisco. The fortunes of irredentists resulted from the continual flow of money and people between Italy and San Francisco. Among pragmatists, ethnic identity was crucial in persuading Italians that California could be a transplanted Italy and that immigrants should rely on influential businessmen-compatriots in obtaining their goals. Both factions needed to maintain intact some sense of colony. But, as changing concepts of charity illustrate, approaching colony life from the perspective of local business interests eventually affected even symbolic adherence to Italy's social and political causes.

Colonists, irrespective of factions, were always aware of national disasters and political upheavals in their homeland. Calamities invariably stimulated massive fund-raising campaigns among Bay Area expatriates. Nevertheless, Italy's incessant misfortunes eventually clashed with the colony's growing self-indulgence. When the "San Francisco Committee for the Relief of Italians Expelled from Turkey" began raising funds in July 1912, *L'Italia* "expressed the thoughts of the vast majority of San Francisco's Italians in calling for a halt in the colony's" perpetual cycle of fund-raising benefits.[73] Apparently, exclusive

Ron Robin   131

involvement with Italy as a rallying point for group solidarity was losing its practical implications.

Even language, the most prominent bastion of national identity, suffered the consequences of colony re-alignment. To his profound dismay, the Italian ambassador to the United States learned that the offspring of many leading citizens in the San Francisco enclave could not speak their mother tongue.[74] Within this context, the ill-fated September 20 celebrations of 1895 took on an ominous meaning when the illustrious Andrea Sbarboro rose to deliver a speech on "Rome the Capital." The years of his self-imposed exile from his native Liguria had taken their toll. Stuttering and stammering, Sbarboro could not express himself clearly in Italian. Angry rumblings arose from the crowd. The audience was not outraged by his wretched command of the Italian language; it was his lack of urbanity that disturbed them. "Speak in English," they shouted, "we understand it!"[75]

The solitary reliance on a foreign tongue, remnant of an isolated social structure, merely obscured the benefits that one could gain from skillful use of culture. Like language, the celebration of Italian national events, the enshrining of its heroes, or participation in Italian charity drives had shifted according to the local setting. By the turn of the century, San Francisco's Italians were actively revising their perceptions of past, present, and future. For many, colony life still held glorious, if somewhat opaque memories. Veteran colonists, hoping to embalm for posterity the events of their youth, groped for acceptable cultural dimensions which would retain remnants of colony life. For others, the hardships of the past associated with the country of their birth were best forgotten. The present, within the confines of a tightly-knit colony, curtailed ambitions. Within the colony, the shift from Italian cult figures to Italian heroes of American significance manifested a revised sense of identity which, it was hoped, would match the fresh social order of the New World. Outside colony walls, the consequences of this cultural transfiguration were revealed in the reconciliation between the Catholic Church and local Italians as well as through the alignment between working-class newcomers and labor unions. Under these circumstances, ethnic identity among San Francisco's Italians was now maintained on a symbolic level only. Having discarded introspective Italian cult heroes, and having lost control of basic cultural tools such as language, San Francisco's Italians of the early twentieth century now focused on token aspects of identity such as the celebration of an Americanized cult hero, and extravagant replications of Italian funerary customs which were meant to compensate for the decline of Italian ways now isolated in the world of reality.

Figure 15
John Fugazi Mausoleum, Italian Cemetery, Colma.
(Photograph by Marlene Getz)

Figure 16
A Typical Boulevard in the Italian Cemetery, Colma.
(Photograph by Marlene Getz)

Figure 17
Andrea Sbarboro Tomb, Holy Cross Cemetery, Colma.
(Photograph by Marlene Getz)

Figure 18
"The Two Lions."
Front Page Illustration from *L'Italia*, July 4, 1907.

Figure 19
Columbus Landing in America.
L'Italia, October 7, 1912.

Figure 20
Original Structure of SS. Peter's and Paul's, 1884.
From *the Monitor*, January 23, 1904.

Figure 21
Design for new SS. Peter's and Paul's, inaugurated, 1924.
From "The New Church of SS. Peter's and Paul's;
Program of the Celebration" (San Francisco, 1924).

140 Signs of Changes

Notes

1. Erik Erikson, *Childhood and Society* (New Edition, 1963), 285-286.
2. Herbert Gutman, "Work, Culture, and Society in Industrializing America, 1815-1919," *American Historical Review*, 78 (June 1973), 560.
3. Dino Cinel, "Conservative Adventurers; Italian Immigrants in Italy and San Francisco" (Ph.D., Stanford, 1979).
4. Herbert Gans, "Symbolic Ethnicity; The Future of Ethnic Groups and Culture in America," in Herbert Gans et al. (eds.), *On The Making of Americans; Essays in Honor of David Riesman* (Philadelphia, 1979), 193-220.
5. Hans C. Palmer, "Italian Immigration and the Development of California Agriculture," (Ph.D., U.C. Berkeley, 1965), 113.
6. Alberto Meloni, *Italian Americans; a Study Guide and Source Book* (San Francisco, 1978), 82.
7. Consulate of Italy, San Francisco, "Report Number 7--General Affairs," March 3, 1865 (Ms., San Francisco Public Library). Olga Richardson's English translation of the document appears in *California History*, 60 (Winter, 1981-82), 361-367.
8. Palmer, "Italian Immigration," 397, 398.
9. Massimo Livi-Bacci, *L'Immigrazione e L'Assimilazione degli Italiani negli Stati Uniti* (Milano, 1961), 5-10.
10. *Ibid.*, 9-20; Robert Foerster, *The Italian Emigration of Our Time* (Cambridge, Mass., 1926), 390-397.
11. Amy Bernardy, "Sulle Condizione delle Donne e dei Fanciulli Italiani negli Stati Uniti del Centro e dell' Ovest della Confederazione del Nort-America," *Bollettino dell' Emigrazione*, 1 (1911), 22-23.
12. Lorenzo Feraud, *Da Biella a San Francisco di California* (Milano, 1882), 113; Andrew Torrielli, "Italian Opinion on America as Revealed by Italian Travellers; 1850-1900," *Harvard Studies in Romance Languages*, 15 (1962), 22-231, 267.
13. United States Bureau of the Census, *Twelfth Census of the United States, 1900*, 1 (Washington D. C., 1901), clxxix, 739, 802, 887; *Thirteenth Census of the United States*, 7 (Washington, D. C., 1913), 828, 1010
14. Dino Cinel, *From Italy to San Francisco*, 31-32; 141-158.

Ron Robin   141

15. Francesca Loverci, "The Society's Role in the Early History of the Italian Colony," *Societa' Italiana di Mutua Beneficenza; The Early Years* (Colma, Ca., 1983), 11-18.

16. *L'Italia*, September 30, 1901. For an additional example of factional warfare within the established colony see Adolfo Rossi, "Per la Tutela degli Italiani negli Stati Uniti," *Bollettino dell' Emigrazione*, 16 (1902), 124.

17. San Francisco *Call*, June 27, 1894, 1.

18. Ernst Gombrich, *Art and Illusion; a Study in the Psychology of Pictorial Representation* (Princeton, N. J., 1960), 79-90.

19. For a review of Bay Area ethnic cemeteries, including the Italian burial ground, see Mark M. Trembley, "Cemeteries; Diverse Landscape features in the San Francisco-Oakland Metropolitan Area" (M.A., U.C. Berkeley, 1970).

20. J. L. Fischer, "Art Styles as Cultural Cognitive Maps," *American Anthropologist*, 63 (February, 1961), 79-93.

21. Henrie Glassie, *Folk Housing in Middle Virginia* (Knoxville, 1975), 181.

22. Andrea Sbarboro, "La California, la Vera Italia d'America," *Monitore Californiano*, 1 (February-March 1914), 5. On the different attitudes of Sbarboro and Giannini the pragmatists, and Fugazi the irredentist see James and Bessi Marquis, *Biography of a Bank* (New York, 1954), 10-13.

23. S. Abita, M. A. Fusco, *Garibaldi nell' Iconografia dei Suoi Tempi* (Milano, 1982); *Garibaldi; Cento Anni Dopo; Atti del Convegno di Studi Garibaldini* (Firenze, 1983).

24. *L'Italia*, July 4, 1907.

25. *Ibid.*

26. *Ibid.*

27. *Ibid.*, July 4, 1909; July 4, 1910.

28. *Ibid.*, July, 3, 5, 1913.

29. Reid Badger, *The Great American Fair; The World's Columbian Exposition and American Culture* (Chicago, 1979), 43. Charles Speroni, "The Development of the Columbus Day Pageant of San Francisco," *Western Folklore*, 7 (October, 1948), 329. For an example of the rise in Columbus Day celebrations after the decline in the Garibaldi cult see *L'Italia*, October 12, 1913.

30. *L'Italia*, October 10, 1909.

31. *Ibid.*

32. *Ibid.*, April 18, 1926.

142 Signs of Changes

33. Daniel Boorstin, *The Americans; The National Experience*, 49.
34. For a belated yet detailed English-language report on the crisis see *Call*, October 10, 1895, 16; December 9, 1895, 8.
35. *Ibid.*, October 11, 1895, 10.
36. Examples of the mustering of Italian votes for mainstream American political contests are documented in *Call*, June 30, 1896, 11.
37. *Ibid.*
38. The decline of September 20 celebrations in San Francisco is discussed in *L'Italia*, September 13, 1909. The modest alternatives to large, colony-wide celebrations are surveyed in *L'Italia*, September 26, 1911, September 14, 1912, September 18, 19, 1913.
39. *Ibid.*
40. *Ibid*; Ettore Patrizi, *Gli Italiani di San Francisco* (San Francisco, 1911), 20.
41. On Campanalismo see Dino Cinel, *From Italy to San Francisco*, 197, 220-221, 226-227. "Ubi Panis Ibi Patria" was a common reason given for disenchantment with the Italian national state. See Pasquale Villari, "L'emigrazione e le sue consequenze in Italia," *Nuova Antologia*, 132 (Rome, 1907), 53.
42. Images of California and its huge expanse of agricultural territory were popular themes in Italians' perceptions of the state. See Lee Harvey Benson, "Achille Loria's Influence on American Economic Thought, Including his Contribution to the Frontier Hypothesis," *Agricultural History*, 24 (October, 1950), 182-199.
43. Raffaello Cioni (ed.), *Canti Popolari Raccolti nel Mugello* (Borgo di San Lorenzo, Italy, 1928), 36-37.
44. Rossi, "Per la Tutela degli Italiani," 109.
45. Feraud, *Da Biella a San Francisco*, 113 discusses the "white" status of Italians in San Francisco.
46. *L'Italia*, July 29, 1901; Palmer, "Italian Immigration," 143.
47. Guido Rossati, "Condizioni del Lavoro negli Stati Uniti," *Bollettino dell' Emigrazione*, 3 (1907), 66-74. See also Peter Varcados, "Labor and Politics in San Francisco; 1880-1892" (Ph.D., U.C. Berkeley), 96 on general attitudes towards unskilled labor among San Francisco's craftsmen.
48. Edwin Fenton, *Immigrants and Unions; a Case Study; Italians and American Labor, 1870-1920* (New York, 1975), 197-258, 559-578. This iconoclastic study of the relationship between organized labor and Italians deals only with

Ron Robin 143

the east coast experience. On trends in San Francisco see Clara Mortenson, "Organized Labor in San Francisco from 1892 to 1902" (M.Sc., U.C. Berkeley, 1916), 10.

49. For an example of the political activities of Italian mutual aid societies see the report on the Scavengers' Union in the *Call*, November 1, 1898, 7.

50. California State Federation of Labor, *Proceedings of the Seventh Annual Convention* (Stockton, 1907), 87, 91; ---------, *Proceedings of the Eleventh Annual Convention* (Bakersfield, 1911), 69.

51. San Francisco's Italian Newspapers regularly reported on meetings held by this union local. See for example: *L'Italia*, July 3, 1903.

52. Silvano Tomasi, *Piety and Power; The Role of Italian Parishes in the New York Metropolitan Area, 1880-1930* (New York, 1975), 15-43.

53. For an example of the transformation of pagan gods into saints among Italy's peasants see Carlo Levi, *Christ Stopped at Eboli* (New Edition, New York, 1964), 117-121.

54. Silvano Tomasi, "The Ethnic Church," in Silvano Tomasi and Madeline Engels (eds.), *The Italian Experience in the United States* (New York, 1970), 78, 94-95; Harold Abramson, *Ethnic Diversity in Catholic America* (New York, 1973), 10.

55. *Monitor*, September 17, 1878. No page numbers available for this publication.

56. "The Italian Church," *Monitor*, January 23, 1906.

57. Dino Cinel, "Conservative Adventurers; Italian Immigrants in Italy and San Francisco" (Ph.D., Stanford, 1979), 292-293.

58. "National Churches of the Archdiocese," *Monitor*, January, 23, 1904; Tomasi, *Piety and Power*, 61-76.

59. While the Archdiocese avoided mentioning local September 20 celebrations, the anti-Catholic nativist American Protective Association mentioned the event often. See *American Patriot*, September 28, 195, 7.

60. "The New Italian Church of SS. Peter and Paul; Program of the Celebration" (Salesian Brothers, San Francisco, 1924), 15-16.

61. Raymond Dondero, "The Italian Settlement of San Francisco" (M.A., U.C. Berkeley, 1960), 92.

62. "An Era of Church Building," *Monitor*, January 23, 1904.

63. *Ibid*; "National Churches of the Archdiocese."

64. The lot sizes of churches mentioned here are from *Handy Blockbook of San Francisco* (San Francisco, 1894).

144 Signs of Changes

65. *Call*, February 28, 1896.

66. On Transigenti and Intransigenti among Italy's priests see Rudolph Vecoli, "Prelates and Peasants; Italian Immigrants and the Catholic Church," *Journal of Social History*, 2 (Spring 1969), 254-268. On the Salesian Brothers in San Francisco see "The New Italian Church," 39-41.

67. *L'Italia*, September 21, 1908.

68. On the Jesuits in California see John Bernard McGloin, *Jesuits By the Golden Gate* (San Francisco, 1972); Gumina, *The Italians of San Francisco*, 169-163. On the establishment of an additional Italian parish in Ocean View see "The New Church of SS. Peter and Paul," 39.

69. A sketch of this Baroque style edifice appears in the *Monitor--Annual Edition*, January, 1910.

70. "The New Church of SS. Peter and Paul," 33.

71. *Ibid.*

72. On the different attitudes of Sbarboro and Giannini the pragmatists, and Fugazi the irredentist see James and Bessi Marquis, *Biography of a Bank* (New York, 1954), 10-13. The pragmatist urgings to view California as the "New Italy" are discussed in Andrea Sbarboro, "La California, La Vera Italia d'America," *Monitore Californiano*, 1 (Feb-March 1914), 5.

73. *L'Italia*, July 2, 1912.

74. E. Mayor Des Planches, "Atraverso il Continente Nord Americana," *Nuova Antologia*, 132 (November, 1907), 28.

75. *Call*, September 21, 1895, 9.

EPILOGUE

Through the haze of a bleak San Francisco evening in the late 1880s, a young girl gaped at a team of straining horses as they dragged a large house from a nearby working-class neighborhood, past her modestly fashionable street, in the direction of the barren sand dunes at the city's outskirts. "See what they have persuaded me to do," she imagined the house to say, almost apologizing as it reluctantly, but prudently departed from its old, decaying neighborhood towards a wind-swept lot now made reputable by the ever-expanding city.[1]

Although embarrassed for having been discovered during the course of its furtive journey through the comfortable neighborhoods bordering on Van Ness Avenue, the creaking wooden structure accepted its fate as an agreeable compromise between survival and extinction. Erstwhile respectable abodes in the city's blue-collar district south-of-Market, Harriet Lane Levy recalled in her reminiscences, had fallen into disfavor as the city branched out in new directions. Only those houses survived that lurched in the direction of urban progress.

Of course, all was not lost by surrendering to the inevitable. Identity could be maintained if one accepted modest re-orientation. "In spite of its fresh coat of paint" and new surroundings, the versatile house rumbling through the city streets "would not be permitted to forget its history."[2] In a city well attuned to change, this striking display of adaptability and mobility typified the compromises made by urbanites caught between their customary needs and an often enigmatic process of urbanization.

Expedient solutions for urgent urban predicaments characterized city life in the United States. The experience of change, coupled with the need to reduce movement to manageable proportions, encouraged city dwellers to stress the portable elements of their culture. San Franciscans, Like Harriet Lane Levy's house, adapted to unforseen circumstances by clinging to familiar essentials and relinquishing what they perceived to be transitory.

The preceding pages have focused on unfathoming this malleable concept of culture by examining visual rather than written records. Given the narrow segment of society endowed with the opportunity to articulate their thoughts in English, I have sought to follow the interaction of ideas taking place through the medium of signs and symbols. Two basic sets of collective representations have been analyzed here: that of mainstream, English-speaking San Francisco, and reflections on urban culture as articulated by European immigrants. Some solid

146   Signs of Changes

common denominators emerge from what appears to be an extremely varied meshing of sources and people. Perhaps the most important collective attribute of the material examined here, is that in no case does the art work of these various human particles of the urban world appear to be either a simple glorification of some privileged class or reclusive reflections of an introspective world of one of urban America's various sub-cultures.

Even the municipally-sponsored art work of politicians, such as representations of the Forty-niner in San Francisco, cannot be approached as merely a tool for serving the ideological interests of his middle-class creators. Instead, the miner's changing appearance, the company he kept, and his surroundings, reflected the increasing complexity of the urban infrastructure in which he was implanted. From an ordinary, individual workingman, totally pre-occupied with the economic opportunities of an unrestricted environment, the miner gradually shed his identification with any particular class or ethnic group. Instead, he eventually took upon himself the task of representing the intricate matrix of interdependencies of the urban setting, the machine-like qualities of contemporary life, in which the functioning of all the elements in the urban apparatus were reliant upon the smooth functioning of all the other cogs. The various images of the Forty-niner as portrayed in the thirty-five year period examined in this book did not derive from a unified set of beliefs that one group had imposed on another. No over-arching ideology, no singular attempt at class domination emerges from an examination of the iconography of the California miner. The catalyst for shifts in the iconography of the Forty-niner appears related to the changing texture of the urban infrastructure, in particular, San Francisco's transition from boomtown to an integral part of the multi-layered, interdependent, urban industrial complex.

The cultural signs of this archetype of municipal art in San Francisco match the symbolism inherent in immigrant forms of visual expressions of communal identity in the city. To be sure, immigrant symbols in San Francisco appear, at first glance, to belong to an intra-communal world far removed from the image of the Forty-niner in mainstream civic art. However, the ostensibly ethnocentric motifs in the iconography of immigrants should be understood as an alternative visual syntax rather than an indication of alien content. The articulation of unfamiliar concepts demands the use of a familiar form which in no way dictates its inherent significance. Consequently, the idioms of ethnic visual expressions in

San Francisco were derived from the internal world of the respective sub-groups examined here, but their content was peculiarly American.

Indeed, it is possible to discover a distinctly American relevance even in the most private spheres of local immigrant ways in San Francisco, as demonstrated by the analysis of the city's Italian cemetery. Although local funeral sanctuaries were modeled on distant Italian customs, their content mirrored many of the curious characteristics of American urban life. An analysis of the art work of the tombs, in particular the juxtaposition of the repetitive art patterns of egalitarian societies, with the elaborate configurations of elitist leanings, was typical of the habitual disposition of American society to fuse opposites, and blend what appeared to be mutually insoluble formulas.

In the more public sphere of communal symbols among San Francisco's Italians we find much worshiping of explicitly Italian heroes, refashioned to meet local conditions. The two most important figures were the Italian adventurer, Christopher Columbus, and the Risorgimento hero, Giuseppe Garibaldi, an almost mythical immigrant, warrior, and ardent Italian patriot. Both figures were integral parts of the hagiography of the nascent Italian political entity, and, as such, constituted an innate part of the immigrant cultural baggage. Yet, in many ways, the messages embedded in the San Francisco versions of these figures and the relationship between them reflected a strikingly American set of concerns.

In Italy, Giuseppe Garibaldi was depicted in vivid, lively scenes of battle, camaraderie, and suffering; he personified Italy's struggle for national unity, and his images glorified those who had appropriated the reins of power in the aftermath of national unity. In San Francisco, Garibaldi's representations were of a more individual and abstract quality. Neutral, white backgrounds, and the lack of significant others removed him from a firmly-anchored historical setting. The subsequent juxtaposition of the Italian figure with symbols of American virtues, such as his coupling with George Washington, signaled the dilution of an exclusive sense of otherness among San Francisco's Italians.

Garibaldi retained his dominant position as cardinal colony symbol during that particular episode in San Francisco history in which the gold-rush mentality of private, unfettered initiative, and inner-directed moral and economic behavior dominated people's lives. With the demise of the gold rush, the standardization of economic activity, and a growing awareness of the unavoidable mutual dependencies of industrial society, the figure of Garibaldi was eclipsed by the hitherto modest role-model, Christopher Columbus. Much of Columbus's

148   Signs of Changes

attractiveness was related to his iconographic legibility, for in many ways he assumed the characteristics of the popular American pioneer in general, as well as the local, San Francisco version of the American frontier spirit, the Forty-niner. Much like the Forty-niner, the local version of Christopher Columbus was presented within the context of belonging to a group of discoverers rather than as a solitary adventurer.

The celebration of these two Italian heroes in a foreign context, the evolution of their peculiarly local versions and their shifting fortunes are vivid demonstrations of the selective nature of historic memory in a modern, industrializing society. Italian iconography in San Francisco demonstrates the criteria by which selective symbolic elements are extracted from the vast reservoir of potential historical emblems. Even though Garibaldi and Columbus were genuine historical figures, their resonance was derived less from the reality of their personal past than their high degree of recognition and from the correspondence of their perceived characteristics to a contemporary predicament. They fulfilled the role of explaining unfamiliar phenomena in familiar terms. As such, the longevity and modification of their public images in San Francisco were by-products of shifts in local social forms and systems of values.

This creative use of history, in which synthesized legends of a real or imaginary past were used to make sense out of unfamiliar predicaments, was part and parcel of the Jewish iconographic repertoire in San Francisco, too. During the loosely-structured gold-rush period, in which eccentric individualism was tolerated and personal material accomplishments were much admired, the architecture of Hebrew temples in San Francisco celebrated both. Temple Emanu-El, the flagship of Jewish identity, was boldly foreign and materialistically ostentatious. Standardization within the economic and social realms triggered an analogous transformation of overt Jewish identity, as reflected in the ceremonial architecture of prominent synagogues and temples. The generic house of worship which succeeded the opulent, ethnocentric temples of a preceding era transformed diversity into unity. The old temple had reflected the subtle confusion of attitudes which had characterized the private city; the new generation of standardized temples in the early twentieth century attempted to meet the demand for stock images in a city which now partook of the continental urban network.

Jewish ecclesiastic architecture ultimately ventured a step further by attempting to produce a synthetic sense of pseudo-historical communal identity. In many ways, this vogue of mission-style synagogues, comprising bric-a-brac

Ron Robin 149

styles, and a confusion of religious and communal function were by-products of life in a modern industrial society. The architecture was composed of seemingly incongruous Jewish and Hispanic elements. But, like the process of assembly line production, in which seemingly unrelated particles were produced separately and without any overt clues regarding their eventual assembling into one unit, so too, the connection between Judaism and a Hispanic-Catholic pristine California was far from obvious. The ultimate architectural fusion between these independent elements was characteristic of the new symbiosis of urban culture, a uniting of old and new, reality and fantasy, local and foreign into an interlocking composite which highlighted common grounds over differences.

The most vibrant aspect of culture in the American city was its predilection for change and innovation, not the generational transferral of usable values and cherished mores. "By culture we mean those social values and behavioral patterns characteristic of a society, nation, tribe, ethnic group, or the like that will be handed down to and understood by future generations," Richard Beringer notes in his survey of historical analysis.[3] But San Franciscans during this period of urban expansion were neither nation, nor tribe, nor of homogeneous origin; worldviews and ways of life needed to be created, not remembered and passed down. In a swift, machine-like fashion, guidelines for pressing problems were manufactured expediently out of the variety of materials at hand, only to be discarded ruthlessly with the appearance of new, more important issues. Even though certain indigenous elements were maintained, the survival of these transplanted items mainly functioned as a familiar language for the expression of unfamiliar concepts.

This transition in the significance and function of culture was related directly to the socio-economic transmutation of the urban texture, from an uneven assortment of "private" cities with no apparent external guiding principles, to a standardized continental network of interconnected wheels in which paradoxical processes of interaction, opposition, and fusion happened simultaneously. It was, according to art historian, Barbara Novak, a new "age of mechanized speed and power, in which a Newtonian world was, as we are so frequently reminded, replaced by Einsteinian relativity."[4]

If, at times, the implications of this perpetual restiveness have been unclear, we need only cast a glance at the multitude of visual signs of culture, private and public, immigrant or mainstream, for clarification. Through the medium of icons—a relatively unambiguous device for articulating culture in a polyglot ambience—urbanites have denoted their understanding of their enigmatic surroundings. San Franciscans, immigrants and native-born Americans, were continuously called upon to come to terms with expansion, change, confusion, regimentation. The shifting symbolism of their urban iconographies document the method by which city people approached the interweaving contradictions and the inherent ambiguity of their surroundings.

Ron Robin 151

Notes

1. Harriet Lane Levy, *920 O'Farrell Street* (New York, 1937), 11.
2. *Ibid.*, 2-3, 11.
3. Richard Beringer, *Historical Analysis; Contemporary Approaches to Clio's Craft* (New York, 1978), 27.
4. Barbara Novak, *American Painting of the Nineteenth Century; Realism, Idealism, and the American Experience* (New York, 1979), 262.

BIBLIOGRAPHICAL ESSAY

The Analysis of Visual Sources:

My interest in iconography was stimulated by the use of visual material among medieval historians who are often confronted with a lack of written sources. A good point of departure and an excellent example of utilizing visual material within a sparsely-documented medieval context is Walter Horn and Ernest Born, *The Plan of St. Gall; a Study of the Architecture and Economy of, and Life in a Paradigmatic Carolingian Monastery*. 3 Vols. (Berkeley, 1979). Maurice Agulhon, *Marianne into Battle; Republican Imagery and Symbolism in France, 1789-1880* (Cambridge, England, 1981) provides an exemplary intermeshing of visual sources with political and social history in a modern urban context. Amos Rapaport, *The Meaning of the Built Environment; a Nonverbal Communication Approach* (Beverly Hills, 1982) and two studies by Kevin Lynch, *Image of the City* (Cambridge, Mass., 1960) and, *What Time is This Place?* (Cambridge, Mass., 1972) are comparative studies of perceptual objects within an urban setting. A number of recent analyses of photography have broadened my understanding of the visual artifact: David Nye, *Image Worlds; Corporate Identities at General Electric, 1890-1930* (Cambridge, Mass., 1985), Peter Bacon Hales, *Silver Cities; The Photography of American Urbanization; 1839-1915* (Philadelphia, 1984), and Allen Trachtenberg, "Image and Ideology; New York in the Photographer's Eye," *Journal of Urban History*, 10 (August, 1984), provided important guidelines for reading photographs as a historical record.

Anselm Strauss's classic study, *Images of the American City* (New York, 1961) fulfilled the role of an old and trustworthy guide throughout this study. Sam Bass Warner Jr., "Slums and Skyscrapers; Urban Images, Symbols and Ideology," in Lloyd Rodwin and Robert Hollister (eds.), *Cities of the Mind; Images and Themes of the City in the Social Sciences* (New York, 1984), expands on some of Strauss's major points. A wonderful introduction into the the the world of cues and clues for reading land scape and cityscape is Donald Meinig (ed.), *The Interpretation of Ordinary Landscapes; Geographical Essays* (New York, 1979), which contains essays by some of the major figures in cultural and historical geography, including J. B. Jackson, David Lowenthal, Pierce Lewis, and Yi-Fu Tuan.

Ron Robin

Cityscape

I have familiarized myself with the American cityscape by extensive ramblings throughout the city of San Francisco, from its majestic peaks to the graveyards and cemeteries situated in the funeral town of Colma. In deciphering the many symbols engraved in buildings and tombstones, I relied on Arnold Whittick, *Symbols, Signs and their Meaning* (Newton, Mass., 1961) and Edwin Sherman (ed.), *Fifty Years of Masonry in California* (San Francisco, 1898). The variety of burial customs in the San Francisco Bay area is the subject of Mark M. Trembly, "Cemeteries; Diverse Landscape Features in the San Francisco-Oakland Metropolitan Area" (M.A. Thesis, U.C. Berkeley, 1970). In identifying changes in San Francisco's urban morphology between two centuries, I have relied on the Sanborn Insurance Maps of the city. These maps resemble aerial photographs in their detailed dissections of city neighborhoods. Through color codes and a variety of topographical symbols, the shapes, building materials, plumbing, and energy resources of the city are documented in this multi-volume collection which is available at the Bancroft Library, at the University of California Campus, Berkeley. I gained a sense of San Francisco's changing cityscape in the nineteenth century from Frank Marryot, *Mountains and Molehills, or Recollections of a Burnt Journal* (New York, 1855); Harvey Rice, *Letters From the Pacific Slope, or: First Impressions* (New York, 1870); Frank Le Couvreur, *From East Prussia to the Golden Gate* (New York, 1906); Robert Louis Stevenson and Lloyd Osborne, *The Wrecker* (New York, 1892), and Stevenson's 1895 article, "San Francisco," in James D. Hart (ed.), *From Scotland to Silverado. By Robert Louis Stevenson* (Cambridge, Mass., 1966).

I gained some perspective as to trends in urban architecture at the turn of the century through the pages of *Architectural Record*. I broadened my knowledge of California trends in the *California Architect and Building News*. Pictures allowed me to reconstruct the vanishing landscape of urban America. In the Bay Area, I delved into the extensive picture collections at the Bancroft Library, the San Francisco Room at the San Francisco Public Library, and the archives of the California Historical Society in San Francisco. As for other American cities, I leafed through the plethora of picture books on Urban America from David Lowe, *Lost Chicago* (Boston, 1975) to John Grafton, *New York in the Nineteenth Century; 321 Engravings From Harper's Weekly* (New York, 1977). I gained much from the monumental work of I. N. Phelps Stokes, *Iconography of Manhattan, 6*

154   Signs of Changes

vols. (New York, 1915-1928), as well as Moses King, *King's Views of New York, 1896-191, and Brooklyn, 1905* (Reprint, Arno Press, New York, 1980)

William Jordy and Ralph Coe (eds.), *American Architecture and Other Writings by Montgomery Schuyler* (Cambridge, Ma., 1961) is an invaluable collection of late nineteenth century architectural comments by a perceptive contemporary. A historical analysis of trends in California architecture is the subject of Harold Kirker, *California's Architectural Frontier; Style and Tradition in the Nineteenth Century* (San Marino, Ca., 1960). As far as understanding vernacular architecture is concerned, an invaluable guide is Henry Glassie, *Folk Housing in Middle Virginia; A Structural Analysis of Historic Artifacts* (Knoxville, 1975). In treating World Fairs as integral components of cityscape, I found both detail and expository analysis in Reid Badger, *The Great American Fair; The World's Columbian Exposition and American Culture* (Chicago, 1979). Burton Benedict, *The Anthropology of World's Fairs; San Francisco's Panama-Pacific International Exposition of 1915* (Berkeley, 1983) is a collection of articles on San Francisco's most significant international exposition. The official history of the P.P.I.E. is Frank M. Todd, *The Story of the Exposition*, 5 vols. (New York, 1921). Other helpful guidebooks to the fair are Juliet James, *Sculpture and Mural Decorations of the Exposition Palaces and Courts* (San Francisco, 1915); George Perry Stella, *The Sculpture and Mural Decorations of the Exposition* (San Francisco, 1915); Sheldon Cheney, *An Art Lover's Guide to the Exposition* (Berkeley, 1915); John D. Barry, *The City of Domes--A Walk with an Architect About the Courts and Palaces of the Panama-Pacific International Exposition* (San Francisco, 1915); John Trusk and J. Nilsen Lauvrick, *Catalogue De Luxe of the Department of Fine Arts, Panama Pacific Exposition* (San Francisco, 1915); *California's Magazine Special Edition on Art in California* (San Francisco, 1915); Eugene Neuhaus, *The Art of the Exposition* (San Francisco, 1915); Porter Garnett, *The Inscriptions at the Panama Pacific International Exposition* (San Francisco, 1915).

Unearthing the significance of statues and other aspects of public art in Fin de Siecle San Francisco was facilitated through contemporary descriptions such as: Douglas Tilden, "Description of Admission Day Fountain," in San Francisco Board of Supervisors, *Municipal Reports, 1896-1897*, appendix, 392; Society of California Pioneers, *Ceremony of the Unveiling of the Lick Bronze Statuary...* (San Francisco, 1894). Both publications maybe found in the Bancroft Library. The wealth of studies on municipal art throughout the country allowed me to

Ron Robin

compare local San Francisco fashion with national trends. Among the many books on this particular subject I found the following most helpful: J. Sanford Saltus, *Statues of New York* (New York, 1923); Dennis Nawrochi, *Art in Detroit Public Places* (Detroit, 1980); Marilyn Evert and Vernon Gay, *Discovering Pittsburgh's Sculpture* (Pittsburgh, 1983); Ira Bach and Mary Lackritz Gray, *A Guide to Chicago's Public Sculpture* (Chicago, 1983).

As for the abortive plans of the City Beautiful Movement, in particular the imperial designs for the rehabilitation of San Francisco, a host of articles in *Municipal Affairs* and *Chautaquan* between 1890 and 1915 deal with this subject. The proposed guidelines for San Francisco's rehabilitation are expounded by their chief instigator, the architect Daniel Burnham, in Daniel Burnham and Edward Bennett, *Report on a Plan for San Francisco* (San Francisco, 1905). San Francisco's coming to terms with the limitations of the Burnham plan are discussed in Herbert Crowly, "The Promised City of San Francisco," *Architectural Record*, 19 (June, 1906) and "Report of Marsden Manson to the Mayor and Committee on Reconstruction..." (Ms., Bancroft Library, 1906). Burnham's biography and architectural philosophy is documented in Thomas Hines, *Burnham of Chicago; Architect and Planner* (New York, 1974). The differences between Burnham's imperial visions and the modest expectations of local architects are expounded in Charles Augustus Keeler, *The Simple Home* (San Francisco, 1904) and the short-lived periodical *Art and Architecture*. In addition to describing the politics behind the rehabilitation of San Francisco in 1906, Judd Kahn, *Imperial San Francisco; Politics and Planning in an American City, 1897-1906* (Lincoln Nebraska, 1979) also suggests an interesting theoretical model for understanding the nature of urban renovation in general. The standard-bearer of prudent cityscape in the San Francisco Bay Area at the turn of the century was Bernard Maybeck whose contribution to American architecture is documented in Kenneth Cardwell, *Bernard Maybeck; Artisan, Architect, Artist* (Santa Barbara, 1977). Richard W. Longstreth (ed.), *A Matter of Taste; Willis Polk's Writings on Architecture in the Wave* (San Francisco, 1979) unveils the philosophy of another important architect who lived and worked in the Bay Area. The many picture books and descriptions romanticizing San Francisco's plight and prospects in the wake of the 1906 earthquake and fire provide invaluable glimpses of expectations from cityscape. Of particular interest are, Andrew Park, *The City Beautiful; San Francisco Past, Present, and Future* (Los Angeles, 1906); Louis John Stellman, *The Vanished Ruin Era; San*

156   Signs of Changes

Francisco's Classic Artistry of Ruin Depicted in Picture and Song (San Francisco, 1910); Phoenix Photo Company, Scenes of the San Francisco Fire and Earthquake (San Francisco, 1906).

City Life.

The urban observations of James Bryce, *American Commonwealth*, 2vols. (New York, 1888) and the book's many revisions provide an essential point of departure for any study of the American city. Bryce's book also contains an unusually extensive discussion of San Francisco in particular, and California in general. San Francisco also caught the attention of another perceptive Englishman, Rudyard Kipling, whose observations appear in Arrell M. Gibson (ed.), *Rudyard Kipling's West; American Notes by Rudyard Kipling* (Norman Ok., 1981). Of far less notoriety, but also extremely helpful is Amy Bernardy, *America Vissuta* (Turin, Italy, 1911). This detailed travel log by one of Italy's pioneering social uplifters deals with San Francisco, too. The observations of another Italian, Alberto Pecorini, *Gli Americani nella Vita Moderna Osservati da un Italiano* (Milan, Italy, 1909) were helpful, too.

Adna Ferrin Weber, *The Growth of Cities in the Nineteenth Century* (New York, 1899) is a perceptive statistical study of urbanization by a contemporary observer. The census reports of the United States Bureau of the Census strengthened my convictions that, despite obvious differences, San Francisco resembled other metropolitan centers. Particularly helpful were the Census Bureau's many summary volumes such as, *Report on the Social Statistics of Cities in the United States at the Eleventh Census, 1890* (Washington, D.C., 1892), the *Statistical Atlas of the Twelfth Census,* 1900 (Washington, D.C., 1903), and *Abstract of the Thirteenth Census, 1910* (Washington, D.C., 1913). The stimulating works of Louis Mumford, in particular *The City in History* (New York, 1961) and his discussion of art and architecture in *The Brown Decades; A Study of the Arts in America; 1865-1895* (New York, 1931) sparked many of the thoughts traced in this monograph. Arthur M. Schlesinger, *The Rise of the City, 1878-1890* (New York, 1933) introduced me to the lives of ordinary people as important sources of urban history in the United States. Gunther Barth, *City People* (New York, 1980), broadened my understanding of city life beyond the familiar accounts of strife and alienation. Thomas Bender, *Towards an Urban Vision; Ideas and Institutions in Nineteenth-Century America* (Lexington, Kentucky, 1975), although focusing on an earlier period than my particular work,

Ron Robin   157

suggests that the classifying of responses into rigid pro-urban or anti-urban categories obscures more than it reveals about concepts of urban life. The articles in Oscar Handlin and John Burchard (eds.), *The Historian and the City* (Cambridge, Mass., 1963), provide inter-disciplinary perspectives of the urban phenomenon. Morton Keller, *Affairs of State; Public Life in Late Nineteenth Century America*d (Cambridge, Mass., 1977) furnishes the necessary political and institutional background for understanding the significance of city life in the United States. Robert Wiebe, *The Search for Order, 1877-1920* (New York, 1967) suggests that city life represented a complete break from the "island community" mores of America's rural background, while his more convincing work, *The Segmented Society; an Introduction to the Meaning of America* (New York, 1975) describes how city people came to terms with a fragmented and complicated urban world at the turn of the century.

The San Francisco context of urban life is analyzed in Gunther Barth, *Instant Cities; Urbanization and the Rise of San Francisco and Denver* (New York, 1975). Peter R. Decker, *Fortunes and Failures; White-Collar Mobility in Nineteenth Century San Francisco* (Cambridge, Mass. 1978) provides statistical verification for the theme of tenuous social life described in *Instant Cities*. A highly personal analysis of San Francisco's upper crust as reflection of the region's history is the subject of Kevin Starr, *Americans and the California Dream, 1850-1915* (Santa Barbara, Ca., 1981). Douglas H. Daniels, *Pioneer Urbanites; a Social and Cultural History of Blacks in San Francisco* (Philadelphia, 1980), is an lucid commentary on urban life in the Bay Area above and beyond the introspective experiences of blacks. As for city politics in San Francisco, a number of excellent books deal with boss rule, the most important of which are William A. Bullough, *The Blind Boss and his City; Christopher Augustine Buckley and Nineteenth Century San Francisco* (Berkeley, 1979); Walton Bean, *Boss Ruef's San Francisco* (Berkeley, 1972). A revisionist approach to typical historical assessments of Boss rule in San Francisco appears in James P. Walsh, "Abe Ruef Was Not a Boss; Machine Politics, Reform, and San Francisco," *California Historical Quarterly*, 51 (Spring, 1972). George Mowry, *The California Progressives* (Berkeley, 1951), analyzes both the background and the political legacy of California's civic-minded business class, although his characterization of the Progressives as being overwhelmingly white and Protestant is incorrect. Mowry neglects the importance of women and Jews in the Progressive movement. The life and times of the city's colorful Mayor James Rolph are the subject of Herman Goldbeck, "The Political

158 Signs of Changes

Career of James Rolph Jr." (M.A. Thesis, U.C. Berkeley, 1936); David Wooster Taylor, *The Life of James Rolph Jr.* (San Francisco, 1934). As for Reform Mayor James Phelan see, Roy Swanstrom, "The Reform Administration of James D. Phelan, Mayor of San Francisco" (M.A. Thesis, U.C. Berkeley, 1961); Robert Hennings, "James D. Phelan and the Wilson Progressives of California" (Ph.D. Thesis, U.C. Berkeley, 1961). The impact of San Francisco's potent labor movement is described in Robert Knight's, *Industrial Relations in the San Francisco Bay Area, 1900-1918* (Berkeley, 1960) and in lesser detail but with greater analysis in Ira Cross's classic study, *History of the Labor Movement in California* (Berkeley, 1935). An important, though neglected issue in politics at the turn of the century in San Francisco is analyzed in Philip Λ. Kalisch, "The Black Death in Chinatown; Plague and Politics in San Francisco, 1900-1914," *Arizona and the West*, 14 (Summer, 1972). The opinionated John P. Young, *San Francisco, a History of the Pacific Coast Metropolis*, 2 vols., (San Francisco, 1912) is an indispensable reference tool for any study of nineteenth century San Francisco.

My work with primary sources in San Francisco began with the annual San Francisco Board of Supervisors, *Municipal Reports*, a collection of statistics and reports on municipal endeavors within the city. City directories and real estate Block Books highlighted urban patterns of living and the multi-cultural texture of San Francisco's neighborhoods. The burden of leafing through faded newspapers was lightened by the San Francisco *Call's* index reels which cover the period 1894-1903. For the years not covered by the *Call's* index, I turned to the *New York Times* index for a sense of major events in San Francisco, and their national significance. An incomplete index of nineteenth century Oakland newspapers, available at the Oakland Public Library, proved helpful, too. Sporadically, and with the aid of the indexes, I focused my newspaper readings on the San Francisco *Chronicle, Examiner,* and *Call*. As for periodicals, the well illustrated *Wave*, the short stories in the *Overland Monthly*, the booster articles in *Sunset*, and the Progressive Party's *California Outlook* were my main sources. Horatio Alger's "gold series," *The Young Miner; or Tom Nelson in California* (Philadelphia, 1879), *Joe's Luck; A Boy's Adventure in California* (New York, 1887); *Digging for Gold; a Story of California* (Philadelphia, 1892) clarified contemporary impressions concerning gold, luck, and fortune in California. Frank Norris, *The Octopus* (New York, 1910), a thinly-disguised attack on the power of the Southern Pacific Railroad in California, and *Mc Teague; a Story of San*

Ron Robin   159

Francisco (New York, 1900; C. 1899), Norris's tale of distress and hopelessness among San Francisco's ordinary people, capture fascinating glimpses of city life and politics at the turn of the century. I gained much information concerning the working-class in the Bay Area from Jack London, *The Valley of the Moon* (New York, 1913) and *John Barleycorn* (New York, 1913). Elizabeth G. Potter and Mabel Thayer Gray, *The Lure of San Francisco* (San Francisco, 1915) plays upon the vogue of tracing roots to pseudo-hispanic origins, while Joseph A. Dunn, *Carefree San Francisco* (San Francisco, 1905), seeks more cosmopolitan vistas. An indispensable reference tool concerning California literature is Newton D. Baird and Robert Greenwood, *An Annotated Bibliography of California Fiction; 1664-1970* (Georgetown, Ca., 1971). Oral histories of the Bay area were helpful, too. At the Western Jewish Historical Center, at the Judah Magnes Museum, Berkeley, I found J. Lloyd Conrich, "Grandma's Boarding House," and at the Bancroft Library, a series of oral histories compiled by Fredrick M. Wirt, "Growing up in Cities" (Ms., 1977-79) served me quite extensively. Of course, the works of Hubert H. Bancroft are vital points of departure for understanding the life of the city's elite. Of particular interest are the many manuscripts of Bancroft's interviews with San Francisco's business leaders which are on file at the Bancroft Library, and his *Chronicles of the Builders*, 7 vols. (San Francisco, 1892). One cannot approach Bancroft's multi-voluminous writings without referring to his insightful biography, John W. Caughey, *Hubert Howe Bancroft; Historian of the West* (New York, 1946).

Immigrants.
Any study of immigrants in California between two centuries inevitably gravitates towards the papers and correspondence of Simon Lubin at the Bancroft Library. As founder and Chief Commissioner of the California State Commission on Immigration and Housing (hereafter: CIH), his private files contained copies of practically all the correspondence that passed through the Commission. Additional material concerning the Commission may be found in the correspondence of the California Department of Industrial Relations--Division of Immigration and Housing, also on file at the Bancroft Library. The personal papers of Simon Lubin's father and one of California's most important businessmen-reformers, David Lubin, are stored at the Western Jewish Historical Center, Judah Magnes Museum, Berkeley. The papers of University of California history professor, Bernard Moses, deal extensively with perceptions and attitudes

160   Signs of Changes

towards minorities and immigrants in California at the turn of the century. The
CIH, Annual Reports and their other important publications, *An A. B. C. of
Housing* (Sacramento, 1915), *Report on Relief of Destitute Unemployed, 1914-1915*
(Sacramento, 1915), and *The Home Teacher; The Act, With a Working Plan for
Forty Lessons* (Sacramento, 1916), detail the philosophy and working
arrangements of the Commission. The Biennial Reports published by the
California Bureau of Labor Statistics from 1883 onwards deal extensively with
immigrants, too. The articles in the short-lived periodical *Immigrant in America
Review*, edited by Simon Lubin's mentor, Frances Kellor, provides a national
perspective through its reviewing of similar commissions in other states. The
articles assembled in Frank B. Lenz, *Immigration; Some New Phases of the
Problem* (San Francisco, 1915) are from a conference on immigration held at the
Panama-Pacific International Exposition. Of interest too, is the oral history of
CIH Commissioner Paul Scharrenberg, "Reminiscences" (Ms., Bancroft Library),
and Charles Blanpied, *A Humanitarian Study of the Coming Immigration Problem
on the Pacific Coast* (San Francisco, 1913).

The standard monograph on the CIH is Samuel E. Wood, "The California
State Commission of Immigration and Housing; a Study of Administrative
Organization" (Ph.D. Thesis, U.C. Berkeley, 1942). Spencer J. Olin's, "European
Immigrants and Oriental Aliens; Acceptance and Rejection by the California
Legislature of 1913," *Pacific Historical Review*, 35 (August, 1966) was helpful, too.
As for attitudes concerning the largest groups of immigrants in California, the
background for anti-Chinese sentiments and the makeup of the local Chinese
community is analyzed in Gunther Barth, *Bitter Strength; A History of the
Chinese in the United States; 1850-1870* (Cambridge, Mass., 1964). Alexander
Saxton, *The Indispensable Enemy; Labor and the Anti-Chinese Movement in
California* (Berkeley, 1971) describes the pressures leading to anti-Chinese
prejudices. I have relied on Roger D. Daniels, *The Politics of Prejudice; The
Anti-Japanese Movement in California and the Struggle for Japanese Exclusion*
(Berkeley, 1962) for an understanding of anti-Japanese sentiment. Both Daniels
and Saxton use as their point of departure the concept of xenophobia suggested
in John Higham, *Strangers in the Land; Patterns in American Nativism 1860-1925*
(Rutgers, N. J., 1963). The title of David Herman, "Neighbors on the Golden
Mountain; The Americanization of Immigrants in California; Public Instruction
as an Agent of Ethnic Assimilation; 1850-1933" (Ph.D. Thesis, U.C. Berkeley,

Ron Robin 161

1981) does not reveal the monograph's extensive grapplings with the nature of immigration above and beyond the schoolhouse.

Through the years, the only comprehensive study of San Francisco's Jewry was Michael Zarchin, *Glimpses of Jewish Life in San Francisco* (Oakland, Ca., 1964). A poorly researched Rudolph Glanz, *The Jews of California, from the Discovery of Gold Until 1880* (New York, 1960) did little to clarify some of the neglected issues in Zarchin. Fred Rosenbaum, *Architects of Reform; Congregational and Community Leadership; Emanu-El of San Francisco, 1849-1980* (Berkeley, 1980), while ostensibly a monograph concerning a particular congregation in the city, has challenged some of Zarchin's contentions. Irena Narell, *Our City; The Jews of San Francisco* (San Diego, 1981) is a popular history of the city's Jewry which concentrates on the life and times of old timers. The collection of articles in Moses Rischin, *The Jews of the West; The Metropolitan Years* (Berkeley, 1979) place the San Francisco experience within a broad western context. Norton B. Stern, *California Jewish History; a Descriptive Bibliography* (Glendale, California, 1967) is the most comprehensive bibliographical aid available.

Among the published works of contemporaries, Jacob Voorsanger, *The Chronicles of Emanu-El* (San Francisco, 1900) illuminates the life of the community's great men. Martin Meyer, *Western Jewry; an Account of the Achievements of the Jews and Judaism in California* (San Francisco, 1916) is a good example of how local Jews usurped the pioneering tradition in California. A fascinating autobiography by Harriet Lane Levy, *920 O' Farrell Street* (New York, 1937) documents the culture and traditions of the veteran Jewish establishment. Other insights may be gained from the San Francisco observations of Rebekah Kohut, *My Portion (New York, 1925)* , the daughter of Rabbi A. S. Bettleheim who spent some time in San Francisco in the late nineteenth century. The novels of Emma Wolf, in particular, *Heirs of Yesterday* (Chicago, 1900) highlight the assimilation of veteran Jews in the community. An interesting personal account by Mark Gerstle, "Memories" (Ms., Bancroft Library, 1943), illustrates the rise of petty peddlers to the ranks of affluent merchants in San Francisco.

Short stories published in turn-of-the-century San Francisco magazines document the stereotyped image of Jews. For examples see Grant Carpenter, "The Claws of the Dragon; The Official, The Jew, and the Prophet," *Sunset Magazine*, 30 (March 1913), 305-314; Grace Helen Bailey, "The Jew," *Overland*

162   Signs of Changes

Monthly, 45 (March, 1905), 193-195; Frank Norris, "Judy's Service of Gold Plate," in *Frank Norris of The Wave* (San Francisco, 1931), 55-56.

As for primary sources, a well-organized, and excellent resource center is available at the Western Jewish Historical Center, situated at the Judah Magnes Museum, Berkeley (WJHC). Of particular interest is the Eastern European Oral History Project, compiled by archivist Ruth Raphael. The many interviews mentioned in Chapter 3 are from this collection. Numerous microfilm reels from the archives of Congregation Emanu-El are available, too. Jacob Nieto, *Sabbath Eve Service and Hymns and Anthems for Sabbath and Holidays Compiled for Congregation Sherith Israel* (San Francisco, 1899), *Sherith Israel, Prayers, Hymns, and Exercises for the Hebrew and Religious School of the Congregation Sherith Israel* (San Francisco, 1879), and Jacob Voorsanger, *Ritual for Friday Evening Service* (San Francisco, N. D.) present examples of change in ritual adopted by veteran Jews in the city. The Annual Report of the Emanu-El Sisterhood, and the San Francisco Federation of Jewish Charities, Annual Reports document the work of Jewish uplifters in the city, and their attitudes towards newcomers. All the documents mentioned above may be found at WJHC. The center also publishes a periodical, *Western States Jewish Historical Quarterly.* Both Emanu-El and Congregation Sherith Israel have extensive and accessible archival collections of their own. The temple buildings themselves are rich in symbolism and iconography. The Bancroft Library and the WJHC have numerous pictures of stylistic changes in these Jewish synagogues dating from the gold rush to the present. As for the architecture of the 1866 version of Temple Emanu-El, I learned much from Allan Temko, "Temple Emanu-El of San Francisco; a Glory of the West," *Commentary*, 26 (August 1958), as well as from an interesting study of synagogue architecture in Poland, Maria Piechotka and Kazimierz Piechotka, *Wooden Synagogues* (Warsaw, Poland, 1959). The weekly editions of the periodical *Emanu-El*--available at both WJHC and the Bancroft Library--provided the basis for my research. The WJHC has an incomplete index for *Emanu-El*. A much neglected publication is the *Jewish Times and Observer*, the organ serving the established congregations not affiliated with Emanu-El. This publication is only available at the Bancroft Library. Sporadic editions of another tabloid, *Public Opinion*, owned and edited by Jewish nativist Isidore Choynski, deal extensively with anti-immigrant sentiments among some segments of the city's established Jewry. The relationship between veteran Jews and newcomers permeates the correspondence between the New York based

Ron Robin   163

Industrial Removal Office and the Hebrew Board of Relief in San Francisco. This material is on file at the WJHC. The efforts to ruralize Jewish newcomers are documented in "The International Society for the Colonization of Russian Jews" (Ms., Bancroft Library, 1891?).

A number of important books and articles helped me establish the national significance of the Jewish experience in San Francisco. Rachel Wischnitzer, *Synagogue Architecture in the United States* (Philadelphia, 1955) classifies the various stylistic trends in Jewish houses of worship. David and Tamar de Sola Pool, *An Old Faith in The New World; Portrait of Shearith Israel, 1654-1954* (New York, 1955), and David De Sola Pool, *Portraits Etched in Stone; Early Jewish Settlers, 1683-1831* (New York, 1952) touch upon the symbolism and iconography in Shearith Israel, New York's oldest Jewish congregation. Nathan Glazer, *American Judaism* (Chicago, 1972) and Moses Rischin, *The Promised City; New York Jews, 1870-1914* (New York, 1970) are essential books for understanding the theological and social evolution of American Judaism. A special edition of the *American Jewish Historical Quarterly* (December 1983), which is dedicated to a re-examination of *The Promised City* provides valuable information on current trends in Jewish historiography. Leon A. Jick, *The Americanization of the Synagogue, 1820-1870* (Hanover, N.H., 1976) focuses on the relationship between Reform Judaism and Americanization. Sheldon M. Neuringer, *American Jewry and United States Immigration Policy, 1881-1952* (New York, 1980) deals extensively with east coast reactions to the arrival of newcomers. The iconoclastic Charles S. Liebman, "Orthodoxy in American Jewish Life," American Jewish Yearbook, 66 (New York, 1965) introduced me to the concept of "nominal orthodoxy" among newcomers, a theme which is developed in Herbert Gans, "Symbolic Ethnicity; The Future of Ethnic Groups," in Herbert Gans et al. (ed.), *On the Making of Americans* (Philadelphia, 1979). Within this context I profited from David Singer, "David Levinsky's Fall; a Note on the Liebman Thesis," *American Quarterly*, 19 (Winter, 1967).

The Italian experience in San Francisco has been researched quite thoroughly. One of the older studies and still perhaps the best, is Hans Christian Palmer, "Italian Immigration and the Development of California Agriculture" (Ph.D. Thesis, U.C. Berkeley, 1965). Dino Cinel, *From Italy to San Francisco; The Immigrant Experience* (Stanford, 1982) is the most comprehensive of recent studies. Cinel focuses on the correlation between the availability of land in Italy and the frequency of return migration. Many mistakes in the footnotes and

164 Signs of Changes

bibliography mar this fine study. Much information on San Francisco's Italians which appeared in Cinel's dissertation, "Conservative Adventurers; Italian Immigrants in Italy and San Francisco" (Ph.D. Thesis, Stanford, 1979) has been deleted from the book. Raymond Dondero, "The Italian Settlement of San Francisco," (M.A. Thesis, U.C. Berkeley, 1960), is an original study of residential patterns among the city's Italians. Deanna Paoli Gumina, *The Italians of San Francisco, 1890-1930* (New York, 1978), is a well researched popular history, and Paul Radin, *The Italians of San Francisco; Their Adjustment and Acculturation* (San Francisco, 1935), is basically a collection of interviews and oral histories. Alessandro Baccari, Vincenza Scarpaci, and Gabriel Zavattaro, *Saints Peter and Paul Church; The Chronicles of "The Italian Cathedral" of The West, 1884-1894* (San Francisco, 1985) is the officially sanctioned history of S S. Peter and Paul, San Francisco's Italian parish. The city's Italian Mutual Aid Society has published two significant collections of articles: *Societa' Italiana di Mutua Beneficenza; The Early Years* (Colma, Ca., 1983), and *Garibaldi and California; Centennial 1882-1982* (Colma, Ca. 1982). Both publications contain articles by Francesca Loverci, who has focused on the archives of the local Italian consulate at the Foreign Ministry in Rome. James and Bessi Marquis, *Biography of a Bank* (New York, 1954) is the history of Amadeo Giannini's Bank of Italy, the present-day Bank of America. An interesting collection of source material is available in the Italo-American collection at the San Francisco Room, Sand Francisco Public Library. Compiled by Andrew Canepa, the collection boasts many gems including a rare photocopy of Lorenzo Feraud, *Da Biella a San Francisco di California* (Milan, Italy, 1882). This autobiographical novel is the story of Italian laborers moving through and working in America's major cities. As for newspapers, a complete set of *L'Italia*, the colony's longest surviving publication, is available at Santa Clara University. A broken file of *L'Italia*, and sporadic issues of the rival *La Voce del Popolo* are available at U.C. Berkeley. Issues of the short-lived, *Monitore Californiano*, a publication of local bankers and realtors aimed at increasing Italian settlements in rural areas of northern California, is available at the Bancroft Library. A crucial publication for any investigation of Italian immigration in the United States is *Bollettino dell' Emigrazione* a periodical published by Commissariato dell' Emigrazione, the Italian government's immigrant regulatory agency. The publication includes investigations into the fate and fortunes of Italian emigrants throughout the world. Much attention is paid to local Italian colonies in American cities,

Ron Robin 165

including San Francisco. A helpful tool for approaching this vast amount of material is Francesco Cordasco, *Italian Mass Emigration; the Exodus of a Latin People; a Bibliographical Guide to the Bollettino dell' Emigrazione, 1902-1927* (Totowa, New Jersey, 1980). Cordasco cheerfully ignores library collections of the *Bollettino* west of the Rockies. In fact, U.C. Berkeley and other institutions in California have complete sets. An additional publication which touches upon the fortunes of Italians in American cities, including San Francisco, is *Italica Gens*, the organ of Italy's missionary priests. To my knowledge only the Catholic University in Washington, D.C. has copies of this periodical. The nature of colony life in San Francisco at the turn of the century is analyzed by the Italian ambassador to the United States in E. Mayor Des Planches, "Attraverso il Continente Nord Americana, " *Nuova Antologia*, 132 (November, 1907). The Italian Geographical Society's *Memorie della Societa' Geografica Italiana; Indageni sulla Emigrazione Italiana all' Estero Fatte per Conte della Stessa Societa, 1888-1890, 4* (Rome, 1890) compares living conditions among Italians in American cities, including San Francisco. Carlo Dondero, *Relazione sugli Italiani della Costa Pacifica* (San Francisco, 1897) conveys a sense of the political feudings among, as well as the prosperity of, San Francisco's Italians. The positive attitude of organized labor towards Italians, particularly in the early decades of the twentieth century is described in detail in the California State Federation of Labor, *Proceedings of the Seventh Annual Convention* (Stockton, 1907), and *Proceedings of the Eleventh Annual Convention* (Bakersfield, 1911). Nevertheless, both Dino Cinel, *From Italy to San Francisco...*, and Robert Knight, *Industrial Relations in the San Francisco Bay Area...*, assume otherwise, perhaps because they do not distinguish between craft unions and the broader phenomenon of trade unions. Assessments of Italian immigrants within the Catholic establishment in San Francisco are alluded to in passing in the anniversary editions and the annual Christmas issues of the *Monitor*, the official organ of the city's Catholic Archdiocese. Short stories and articles concerning San Francisco's Italians appeared regularly in local literary digests. The stereotypical concept of the hot-blooded Italian was behind J. Van Dusen, "Francesca, a Tale of Fisherman's Wharf," *Overland Monthly*, 38 (Feb 1981); David Henry Walken, "The Close of the Day," *ibid.*, 51 (Feb-Mar, 1908); Kathleen Thompson, "Aux Italiens," *ibid.*, 44 (July, 1905); John Coghlan, "A Political Deal," *ibid.*, 46 (Sept 1905).

166 Signs of Changes

Several important books have broadened my perspective of Italian migration beyond the local San Francisco context. The great pioneering work of Robert Foerster, *The Italian Emigration of Our Time* (Cambridge, Mass, 1919) places the arrival of Italians in the United States in a global context. The book was re-issued by Arno Press in 1969. Massimo Livi-Bacci, *L'Immigrazione e L'Assimilazione degli Italiani negli Stati Uniti* (Milano, 1961) is a lucid statistical analysis of Italian migration to the United States. Andrew Torielli, "Italian Opinion on America as Revealed by Italian Travellers; 1850-1900," *Harvard Studies in Romance Languages*, 15 (1962) discusses the impressions of Italian tourists in the United States. Edwin Fenton, *Immigrants and Unions, a Case Study--Italians and American Labor, 1870-1920* (New York, 1975) challenges the assumption that unions and Italians were perennially at odds. Silvano Tomasi, *Piety and Power--The Role of the Italian Parishes in the New York Metropolitan Area, 1880-1930* considers the Catholic Church as an agent of acculturation. Italian priests who accepted the concept of an Italian national entity are the subject of Rudolph J. Vecoli, "Prelates and Peasants; Italian Immigrants and the Catholic Church," *Journal of Social History*, 2 (Spring, 1969). John Briggs, *An Italian Passage; Immigrants to Three American Cities, 1890-1930* (New Haven, 1978) is a lucid discussion of acculturation and assimilation.